WILDERNESS WITHIN

A GUIDED LENT JOURNAL FOR PRAYER AND MEDITATION

SR. JOSEPHINE GARRETT, CSFN

AVE MARIA PRESS AVE Notre Dame, Indiana

Visit our website to find online components, including videos by Sr. Josephine Garrett, to enhance your experience with *Wilderness Within* this Lent. Go to **www.avemariapress.com/ private/page/wilderness-within-resources**.

Nihil Obstat: Reverend Monsignor Michael Heintz, PhD
         Censor Librorum
Imprimatur: Most Reverend Kevin C. Rhoades
         Bishop of Fort Wayne–South Bend
         Given at Fort Wayne, Indiana, on 5 August, 2024

The *Nihil Obstat* and *Imprimatur* are official declarations that a book or pamphlet is free of doctrinal or moral error. No implication is contained therein that those who have granted the *Nihil Obstat* or *Imprimatur* agree with its contents, opinions, or statements expressed.

Implicit Religion Incomplete Sentences © 2016, Peter T. Malinoski, PhD, crisis@ soulsandhearts.com. Used with permission.

Founded in 1865, Ave Maria Press is a ministry of the United States Province of Holy Cross.

www.avemariapress.com

Paperback: ISBN-13 978-1-64680-297-5

E-book: ISBN-13 978-1-64680-298-2

Cover and interior images © 2024 June Jameson, **junejameson.com**.

Cover and text design by Brianna Dombo.

Printed and bound in the United States of America.

CONTENTS

INTRODUCTION

THE WILDERNESS OF THE HEART

ONLY ONCE, PERHAPS, DID THE LORD JESUS REFER TO HIS OWN HEART, IN HIS OWN WORDS. AND HE STRESSED THIS SOLE FEATURE: "GENTLENESS AND LOWLINESS": AS IF HE MEANT THAT IT IS ONLY IN THIS WAY THAT HE WISHES TO CONQUER MAN; THAT BY MEANS OF "GENTLENESS AND LOWLINESS" HE WISHES TO BE THE KING OF HEARTS. THE HEART IS NOT JUST AN ORGAN THAT CONDITIONS THE BIOLOGICAL VITALITY OF MAN. THE HEART IS A SYMBOL. IT SPEAKS OF THE WHOLE INNER MAN. IT SPEAKS OF THE SPIRITUAL INTERIOR OF MAN.

ST. JOHN PAUL II, GENERAL AUDIENCE, WEDNESDAY, JUNE 20, 1979

I believe Lent is not an exceptional time, but rather an exemplary time. It is a time when we enter deeply into the Paschal Mystery, which is at work in us and in the world, not only during the forty days of Lent, but all the time. In this way, Lent becomes an example of what much of the rest of our year and faith journey in general ought to look like.

Preparation for the Resurrection is a lifelong work—a lifelong process of the conversion and transformation of our hearts. Today, we find ourselves here again, at the threshold of Lent, which is really the threshold of our entire faith journey: the process of enthroning God as king in our hearts and in our world, until all things are subjected to him (1 Cor 15:28), including our most inner selves.

Often we hear the idea of the desert or the wilderness as a central theme for the forty days of Lent. The liturgical decorations in our homes and parishes consist of barren branches and dark-purple linens—there is a stark simplicity. This practice is inspired by Matthew 4:1: "Then Jesus was led up by the Spirit into the wilderness to be tempted by the devil." During Lent, we are called to spiritually enter into the wilderness of our hearts with Jesus. In our Lenten observances and sacrifices, we face our temptations head-on with and in Christ because we receive the grace of seeing them more clearly. Our need for God's grace becomes more evident precisely in our intentional efforts to sacrifice.

It seems that almost immediately after we make a resolve to practice any penance or sacrifice or fast, Lenten or otherwise, we are faced with subsequent temptations. St. Augustine helps us frame this as good news: "[Jesus] made us one with him when he chose to be tempted by Satan, he suffered temptation in [our human] nature, but by his own power gained victory for [us]. In him we overcome the devil. He could have kept the devil from himself; but if he were not tempted, he could not teach [us] how to triumph over temptation" (Office of Readings, Commentary on the Psalms). He goes on: "See yourself as tempted, *and* see yourself as victorious," which we can do because Christ has gone before us into the wilderness of the human condition, and now our temptations are faced through him, with him, and in him.

I began writing this journal for you during the Lenten season, and as I looked around at the external signs of the wilderness, I found myself drawn into the interior of my own heart. The cross I wear, which I received on the day of my first vows, bears the inscription, "Ecce Regnum Dei intra vos est." *Behold, the Kingdom of God is in you* (see Luke 17:21). The world seems like a chaotic wilderness, full of opportunities to encounter the enemy and his lies and temptations, but as St. James wrote, "Each person is tempted . . . by his own desire" (Jas 1:14). The sin we see in the world begins in our own hearts. So, I would say, the wilderness into which Jesus is drawn is the wilderness of the human heart, where the sin and evil and suffering we see in the world is conceived.

You and I are the ushers of God's love. As one of my Sisters so wonderfully put it, our job is to incarnate God's love. We are formed to live this mission by allowing God to transform the tangled and untamed wilderness of our hearts into his own so they become fonts and springs of his mercy. As he promises through the prophet Ezekiel: "I will take out of your flesh the heart of stone and give you a heart of flesh" (Ez 36:26).

I recently met with a friend who had a hard time articulating what God wanted to transform in her own heart at this time in her life. She could tell me with precision, decisiveness, and clarity everything she wanted God to transform in her husband and her kids, but when it came to her heart, the clarity seemed to vanish. Her certainty faded as she faced an overwhelming wilderness where the path can seem shadowy and unclear, the terrain unfamiliar. She is a mother, and I think any parent can relate to her. If you are a parent and reading this, you might be thinking, "Sister, when can I find the time to know what is going on in my heart and the areas that Jesus desires to enter into?" And yet, this is probably one of the greatest gifts we can give to our friends, family, and other loved ones—our own growing relationship with Jesus.

Through this journal, we will begin this work by following Jesus as the Spirit drives him into the wilderness (see Mark 1:12). We will travel into the interior wilderness of our hearts, which our Lord seeks to conquer through the gentleness and lowliness of a God who made himself like us so that we could be like him. As St. Athanasius famously said, "The Son of God became man so that we might become God." Jesus's lowliness gives him access to the recesses of our hearts, and his gentleness empowers him to conquer the wilderness without overwhelming us. Before we explore the areas of our hearts in need of healing, we will begin with understanding our hearts by canvassing them and reflecting on how our hearts were made and what they were made for. Then, we will face the realities that plague and burden our hearts and therefore need healing. Next, we will follow Jesus, with our whole hearts, on the road of discipleship and ultimately to the Cross. These are the basics of our faith, ever ancient and ever new, and Lent is the perfect time to return to these fundamentals.

This journey into the wilderness of the heart is not for the purpose of egotistical navel gazing. Rather, by the end of Lent, this journey will help you gather more of your heart up into your hands and offer it to Jesus to enter into, to reign in, to be used for the service of his kingdom, and to be a source of the same divine life that flows from his own Sacred Heart. When we reach Easter Sunday, we will celebrate the gift of Jesus's Resurrection with transformed hearts that look more like his.

Now, let us begin our journey into the wilderness.

HOW TO USE THIS JOURNAL

The *Wilderness Within* Lent journal combines daily meditations, questions for reflection, journaling space, prayers, and beautiful original art to draw you into a deeper, richer experience of Lent. Over the next forty days, you will learn to draw on practical tools from the mental-health field to explore the contours of the human heart and invite Jesus to reign in areas of your heart that may have not been turned over to him. You will also discover how we are all made for relationship, for mission, and for union with Christ.

Every week will have a familiar rhythm. Thursdays are set apart for mental-health check-ins. Why? Because Thursday is the day of the week when Jesus celebrated the Last Supper, so we focus on the Eucharist, the Love of God enfleshed in Christ's Body, Blood, Soul, and Divinity. As a licensed counselor, Sr. Josephine highlights how mental-health skills can help us incarnate the virtues and ultimately incarnate love so we can live Eucharistically.

Each Friday, you will take a moment to pray before either the Holy Face of Jesus or Jesus on the Cross so that when you arrive at Good Friday, you will have already spent some real time with our crucified Lord. Love of the Cross enriches our understanding and experience of the Resurrection.

On the first four Saturdays, we will use a journaling tool that provides an opportunity to look back at and *reverence* the fruit of our reflection, prayer, and experiences on previous days.

Lastly, you are encouraged to plan to go to Confession at least once during Lent. You'll reflect more on Confession during week three, so perhaps you can even schedule an appointment for Confession for that timeframe now.

As we embark on this journey together, we have a unique opportunity set before us to journey with Jesus to the *Wilderness Within* and to follow him to Calvary where we learn to pour ourselves out for mission, in union with Christ. Through the meditations, prayers, scriptures, mental-health tools, and real-life stories in this journal, you will be invited to slow down, to reflect, to prepare, and to create space for daily encounters with Jesus.

WHO IS *WILDERNESS WITHIN* FOR?

Wilderness Within is for anyone who desires to experience the Lenten season as a healing journey that leads you to explore the tangles of your heart so that you can more deeply encounter and embrace God's love and cultivate a life of prayer and service in response. The season of Lent is the ideal time to step back from your life and evaluate where you stand with God, yourself, and others. This journal provides a daily path to prayer and reflection for healing, restoration, and mission.

Wilderness Within was designed for use in a group setting. There's something special about taking this Lent journey with a community, whether that community is your entire parish, a small group, or your family. Visit www.avemariapress.com/private/page/wilderness-within-resources for more information about bulk discounts, a leader's guide, help organizing a small group, videos from Sr. Josephine discussing the theme for each week of Lent, and other resources to help you make the most of your time together with this book.

You can also use *Wilderness Within*'s meditations and journaling prompts on your own to draw nearer to God, hear his voice in new ways, and pour out your soul to him. This journal will help you turn your attention daily to the wilderness of your heart as a place to be explored, restored, and sent on mission by Jesus's tender love. You may find that this Lent you're in special need of regular quiet times of connection with God; *Wilderness Within* is an excellent way to help you find that space each day.

HOW IS *WILDERNESS WITHIN* ORGANIZED?

Wilderness Within is organized into six weeks:

In Week 1, you're called to *begin again* with an earnest desire to live this Lent as a time to deepen your love for God. You'll begin by discovering what it means to *rend your heart* (see Joel 2:13) and open yourself in a spirit of acceptance and curiosity to reveal the wilderness within. This first week might not feel much like Lent, but it will feel like a peeling back, a seeing again, as we assess the ways our hearts have become overgrown and find the courage to enter that wilderness with Jesus.

In Week 2, you'll delve into the purpose of the human heart: relationship. Drawing on the image of the human heart as a garden full of roots, blooms, and brambles in dire need of tending, we will examine the relationships in our lives. Which ones are fruitful? Which ones contain thorns? How do we find a way through? We'll look to the power of baptismal waters and God's refining fire to reveal how we are held in existence by God's love and how holiness and healthy relationships are inextricably linked.

In Week 3, we will do the hard but necessary work of examining the scars on our hearts; how, exactly, are we wounded by sin? This week is your call to humility and repentance, to an honest look at the roots of corporate and personal sin. You'll want to make time for Confession and plan some extra time to conduct a thorough examination of conscience.

In Week 4, you'll begin to see how God designed your heart to be rescued by him. After facing the brokenness that marks each of our hearts, you'll begin to grow in your capacity to be healed and rescued by God. In the garden of your heart, wilderness may seem to rein supreme, yet it is precisely here that God's love burns most brightly.

In Week 5, you will leave the wilderness of your heart so that you can go on mission. Equipped with a heart restored by Christ's love, you are now called to love your neighbor and be a good steward of the gifts and charisms given to you.

In Holy Week, we begin our ascent with Jesus from the Sea of Galilee to Jerusalem to Calvary. You will follow in Jesus's footsteps to the Cross and discover how you can love him well through each stage of the Passion and Resurrection.

Within each week, you'll encounter a simple daily pattern made up of the following parts:

✦ Each day opens with a quotation from a saint, a great teacher, or scripture in order to focus your thoughts on the key idea from that day's meditation.

✦ The meditation draws out a message from scripture, the *Catechism of the Catholic Church*, the field of mental health, and real-life examples that will help you discover the places within that have not yet encountered Christ's love. An important aspect of our Lenten preparation for the Savior is to journey within and see the places that are empty and in need of him so that we can fruitfully turn ourselves right side up to build the kingdom of God on earth.

✦ The reflection challenges you to ponder and journal in response to the meditation, helping you identify practical ways to live out the Christian life more fully. Try to have your Bible nearby so that you can dig into the scripture passages suggested for your prayer time.

✦ Finally, after you've read and journaled, the closing prayer provides a starting point for your own requests and prayers of thanksgiving and praise to God.

HOW SHOULD I READ WILDERNESS WITHIN?

This Lent journal's daily format is flexible enough to accommodate any reader's preferences: If you're a morning person, you may want to start your day with *Wilderness Within*, completing the entire day's reading, reflection, journaling, and prayer first thing in the morning. Or you may prefer to end your day by using *Wilderness Within* to focus your attention on Christ as you begin to rest from the day's activities. You may even decide to read and pray with others in the morning and journal individually in the evening. The key is finding what works for you, ensuring that you have time to read carefully, ponder deeply, write honestly, and connect intimately with the Lord in prayer.

Whatever approach you choose (and whether you decide to experience *Wilderness Within* with a group or on your own), be sure to visit www.avemariapress.com/private/page/wilderness-within-resources for extra resources to help you get the most out of this special Lent journey.

ONLINE RESOURCES

Some of the extra resources offered online at https://www.ave-mariapress.com/private/page/wilderness-within-resources include a Lenten Commitments Check-In, a Guide to Imaginative Prayer, a Handout on Thought Patterns and Distortions, and a Handout on the Physiology of Shame.

 Visit our website to find online components, including videos by Sr. Josephine Garrett, to enhance your experience with *Wilderness Within* this Lent. Go to **www.avemariapress.com/private/page/wilderness-within-resources**.

SOME OF THE REFLECTIONS AND TOPICS IN THE JOURNAL MAY ACTIVATE INTENSE EMOTIONS. IF YOU FIND THAT YOU WOULD LIKE TO RECEIVE SUPPORT FROM A COUNSELOR AND DO NOT HAVE ONE, VISIT **CATHOLICTHERAPISTS.COM** TO LOCATE A COUNSELOR LICENSED IN YOUR STATE.

IN ADDITION, IF YOU NEED MENTAL-HEALTH CRISIS SUPPORT, RESOURCES INCLUDE THE FOLLOWING:

UPPER ROOM CRISIS HOTLINE:
1-888-808-8724
OR
WWW.CATHOLICHOTLINE.ORG

SUICIDE OR CRISIS HOTLINE:
TEXT "HELP" TO **988** OR CALL **988**

WEEK OF ASH
WEDNESDAY

BEGIN AGAIN

WEEK OF ASH WEDNESDAY

ASH WEDNESDAY

OUR LENTEN JOURNEY . . . IS
A JOURNEY ON WHICH EACH
AND EVERY DAY WE LEARN TO
LEAVE BEHIND OUR SELFISHNESS
AND OUR BEING CLOSED IN ON
OURSELVES, TO MAKE ROOM
FOR GOD WHO OPENS AND
TRANSFORMS OUR HEARTS.

POPE BENEDICT XVI, FINAL HOMILY,
FEBRUARY 13, 2013

REND YOUR HEART

After twenty years of being Catholic, I still find myself approaching Ash Wednesday each year with some anxiety and trepidation (even as a nun!). As soon as the day arrives and I begin all my big plans for prayer, fasting, and almsgiving, I find myself immediately fearful of what feels like inevitable failure, as if the purpose of Lent is to "get it right." In reality, I will most likely demonstrate over the next forty days what it looks like to not "get it right." After twenty Lents, I have learned that it takes far more courage to be in a state of beginning again than it does to be in a state of getting it right. Ven. Bruno Lanteri said, "If I should fall even a thousand times a day, a thousand times with *peaceful repentance* I will say immediately *Nunc Coepi* [Now I Begin]." Bl. Mary of Jesus the Good Shepherd—the foundress of my community, Sisters of the Holy Family of Nazareth—said it this way; "Rest assured that the Lord is pleased a thousandfold more by a soul who is susceptible to many falls, but who knowing her weakness, turns to God in humility, than by another who is less prone to fall and is seemingly more perfect, but is self-confident and self-sufficient."

On Ash Wednesday we are instructed in the reading from the prophet Joel to rend our hearts, not our garments (see Joel 2:12). Some of us have heard this time and time again, but have we really understood what the scripture is saying? *Rend* means "to tear." At the outset of Lent, the first instruction from scripture tells us to tear open our hearts before the Lord; I think it's safe to say Lent is not for the folks who seemingly have it all together. Perhaps when we make Lent about mainly checking the boxes of the "things" we said we would do, we have only rended our garments instead of our hearts. Maybe we can reframe these forty days from a journey toward our own perfection to instead a time to strive to have the courage to begin again, and again, again . . . well. In doing so, we can hope to make room for God, who opens (and perhaps it is through his power that this rending happens) and transforms our hearts, for he will only journey into a heart with an open door.

REFLECT

1. Reflect on your own rended heart. If you were to rend (open) your heart before God today, as you enter Lent, what would he find there? Some questions you can ask to help clarify the movements of your heart are "What is stirring in my heart lately?" or "What is breaking my heart lately?"
2. What doubts or anxieties do you have about the forty days ahead? Doubts and anxieties are often attached to desires; what are the desires beneath those doubts and worries?
3. Pray with Romans 5:1–5.

_____

_____

_____

_____

_____

_____

_____

_____

_____

_____

PRAY

_I RETURN TO YOU, LORD, WITH MY
WHOLE HEART. THE PAST IS ASHES,
AND I BRING TO YOU MY TEARS AND
FASTING, TRUSTING THAT YOU ARE
SLOW TO ANGER AND QUICK TO
FORGIVE. AMEN._

WEEK OF ASH WEDNESDAY

THURSDAY

THE FAITHFUL SHOULD THEREFORE ENTER INTO THEMSELVES AND MAKE A TRUE JUDGMENT ON THEIR ATTITUDES OF MIND AND HEART. IF THEY FIND SOME STORE OF LOVE'S FRUIT IN THEIR HEARTS, THEY MUST NOT DOUBT GOD'S PRESENCE WITHIN THEM. IF THEY WOULD INCREASE THEIR CAPACITY TO RECEIVE SO GREAT A GUEST, THEY SHOULD PRACTICE GREATER GENEROSITY IN DOING GOOD, WITH PERSEVERING CHARITY.

POPE ST. LEO THE GREAT, SERMON, FROM THE OFFICE OF READINGS, LITURGY OF THE HOURS, NON-BIBLICAL READINGS FOR LENTEN SEASON

ROCK THE BOAT

A few Ash Wednesdays ago, I was sitting at my desk preparing a guidance-counseling lesson for fifth graders and wondering how to connect our focus on virtuous relationships to the season of Lent. I quickly realized that all Lenten practices (whether prayer, fasting, or almsgiving) ultimately impact some aspect of relationship, hopefully for the better, whether it's relationship with myself, others, or God.

For that guidance lesson, I chose to invite the fifth graders to consider their Lenten plans, reflecting on what relationship(s) would be impacted by fulfilling their commitments. I shared with them that the behaviors of fasting, praying, and giving alms are not ends in and of themselves, but rather paths to virtuous relationships—ways to purify and bring God's power into how we relate to ourselves, others, and ultimately God.

Yesterday, as you sought to rend your heart, I would imagine that what you found there had a lot to do with relationship. You may already have set plans for Lent, and I don't want to stress you out by rocking the boat, inviting some potential adjustment to those plans, and yet, I am going to rock the boat and ask you to reflect on your Lenten plans from this threefold relational perspective. Perhaps you may come away with ideas such as the following: To fast from negative thoughts about yourself, replacing those thoughts with brief prayers. To fast from uncharitable thoughts and gossip about others and strive to presume good will. To regularly spend more time with your family in a common area of your home, or to plan to eat a meal together at the table (so many families no longer practice this simple, yet profound routine that establishes powerful bonds). Or to encounter God more often in the sacrament of Confession, in receiving the Eucharist, or in the Word by opening your Bible more often. Today, take your Lenten plans to God, but in the context of relationship, because that is what you are—a relationship to yourself, to others, and ultimately to God.

REFLECT

1. Reflect on the scripture passage Isaiah 58:6–9.
2. Thinking about what came up yesterday as you opened your heart before the Lord, what do you think God would like to transform in your relationship with yourself, others, or God at this time in your life? Based on what you believe God would like to change, how are you called to pray, fast, and give alms to invite his grace and power in your life so that he can do so? Does this cause a shift in your Lenten plans?
3. What was it like to think of making adjustments to plans you have already discerned for Lent? Sometimes we are very set on doing Lent the way we discerned. What if God would like to evolve that as Lent progresses? Does he have permission?

_____

_____

_____

_____

_____

_____

_____

_____

_____

_____

PRAY

LORD JESUS, WITH YOUR LOVING CARE, GUIDE THE PENANCE I HAVE BEGUN. INSPIRE ME TO SEE YOUR WORK THROUGHOUT IT. HELP ME TO PERSEVERE ACCORDING TO YOUR WILL, WITH LOVE AND SINCERITY IN ALL THINGS. AMEN.

THERE IS NONE LIKE GOD . . .
WHO RIDES THROUGH THE
HEAVENS TO YOUR HELP, AND
IN HIS MAJESTY THROUGH
THE SKIES. O ISRAEL! WHO IS
LIKE YOU, A PEOPLE SAVED BY
THE LORD.

DEUTERONOMY 33:26, 29

JOURNEY INTO THE WILDERNESS

Yesterday's reflection invited us to reframe our Lenten penances as paths to virtuous relationships. In short, prayer, fasting, and almsgiving are not Lent itself. So often we hear, "What are you doing for Lent?" Yet our Lenten plans are not what is being *done* for Lent. Rather, those commitments help us to receive what *Jesus* desires to do *in us* this Lent. It is *God* who accomplishes Lent in us. Today, we dip into the wilderness of our hearts and begin pondering God's work to be done there this Lent.

People often wonder why Jesus needed to go into the wilderness. Some say he had to go in as the "new Adam," in order to restore man's relationship with God through his obedience and trust in God the Father. Some say it was necessary to make more evident Jesus's identity as God's Son. Christ's identity had just been revealed at his baptism; then he enters the wilderness and shows us what living that out looks like. Others instead look to the significance of the wilderness itself, noting the beasts in the wilderness (see Mark 1:13) and considering their presence as a subtle indication that this present wilderness represents what was previously the perfectly ordered Garden of Eden. Now, that wilderness needs to be restored to right order. Those focusing on the wilderness also note the forty years the Israelites spent wandering in the wilderness, dependent on God. The Israelites entered the Jordan River before entering the Promised Land, a place where they hoped to find a new kind of paradise. This is the same river in which Jesus would later be baptized, though he did not depart into the Promised Land afterward.

For our purposes in this journal, we will focus on the wilderness, a place where paths are unpaved, the way is unknown, and what comes next is uncertain. Jesus, then, enters into this place to restore order. So, the short answer to the question of why Jesus goes into the wilderness is simple: *to rescue us.*

Words like *wilderness* and *unknown* tend to conjure emotions such as worry, anxiety, fear, and hesitancy. What if instead we looked to how God has been a faithful provider in the wilderness and trusted that he will do the same for us in the wilderness journey ahead? What if we joyfully take his hand and journey into the wilderness? Because when Christ enters there, "this opposite place of the garden, becomes the place of reconciliation and healing" (Pope Benedict XVI, *Jesus of Nazareth*).

REFLECT

1. What emotions surface for you when you consider going into an unknown, unpredictable place?
2. What shifts in your mind when you contemplate Jesus going into the desert versus going into the wilderness? How does this impact your expectations for the season of Lent?

PRAY

*JESUS, RESCUE ME FROM FEAR AND
TREPIDATION. GIVE ME COURAGE TO
LOOK UPON THE UNKNOWN WITH
JOY AND CURIOSITY. HELP ME TO
FOCUS NOT ON THE TROUBLE IN MY
HEART BUT ON YOU AND THE GIFT OF
YOUR PRESENCE WITHIN ME. BLESS
ME WITH EYES TO SEE AND EARS TO
HEAR AND PERCEIVE YOU, SO THAT
I MAY JOYFULLY PROCLAIM YOUR
RESURRECTION ON EASTER MORNING
AND ALWAYS. AMEN.*

WEEK OF ASH WEDNESDAY

SATURDAY

THE HEART IS OUR HIDDEN
CENTER, BEYOND THE GRASP OF
OUR REASON AND OF OTHERS;
ONLY THE SPIRIT OF GOD CAN
FATHOM THE HUMAN HEART AND
KNOW IT FULLY.

CATECHISM OF THE CATHOLIC CHURCH,
2563

REVERENCE YOUR FINDINGS

It is sometimes said that familiarity breeds contempt. I think this saying needs an important qualifier: *if there is no reverence.* Let me explain. Some say *reverence* means to look again: from the Latin *re* (again) and *ver* (look, see). In that approach, *reverence* means that I keep looking at something, which would imply that there is more to see. Another approach is to examine the alternate Latin etymology: *re* (expressing force) and *vereri* (to fear). *Revereri*, when considered in a biblical sense, is best matched to the Hebrew word *yirah*—a trembling awe.

Etymology aside, when I reflect on some of the biggest mistakes in my life, I recognize that I lacked reverence—a willingness to keep looking, which demands slowing down. I was lacking reverence in my view of another person, of a treasure entrusted to my stewardship, or of an experience of the created world. I failed to see God's presence in it. I think the worst lack of reverence I have participated in is being irreverent toward myself—for the inner workings of my heart and soul as a temple of God. I've learned that the more reverence we have for ourselves, the more likely we are to take time to slow down, find silence, and be still.

I will be frank; I think we are utterly impoverished when it comes to having reverence for ourselves. Pausing and remembering that each of us is a mystical encounter with God; right now in this moment, God is relating to you and to me. Instead we are pedal-to-the-metal as much as is physically possible. We cram our days and our calendars full of activities and events, and then we're puzzled by the lack of meaningful connection in our relationships and marriages. How can I connect with another when I am disconnected from myself?

So, Saturdays in Lent will be days set apart to review our week in conversation with the only One who can really fathom the human heart. We will focus our attention on the week we just completed and take a state of the heart. We will combine St. Ignatius's practice of repetition with a practice I used in the novitiate called "Integration Days." These will be tools to help understand who we are in light of how God sees us and who God is revealing himself to be for us.

REFLECT

1. Place yourself in the presence of God and take on a spirit of receptivity. How has life been for you this week: ordinary or exceptional, messy or tidy, connected or disconnected?

2. How are you feeling about the presence of God in relationships: with yourself, others, and God? Choose one experience that stands out, and reflect:

   ✣ How does this experience remind me of other events in my life?
   ✣ Is there a scripture or maxim (saying) that seems to fit this experience?
   ✣ Is there a pattern or theme in my life that this event relates to?
   ✣ How am I feeling now as I remember it?

3. Listen to the movement within your heart:

   ✣ What is moving now as I reflect on this event?
   ✣ Am I being drawn to something deeper, perhaps gratitude or an action?
   ✣ In general, what is going on inside of me?

_____

_____

_____

_____

_____

_____

_____

_____

_____

_____

PRAY

_LOVING FATHER, GIVE ME THE DESIRE
TO SLOW MY PACE THIS LENT AND
REVEAL TO ME MY LIMITATIONS.
SHOW ME WHERE I NEED TO "LOOK
AGAIN." HUMBLE ME, LORD. AMEN._

FIRST WEEK
OF LENT

A HEART
ROOTED IN LOVE

FIRST WEEK OF LENT

SUNDAY

THEN GOD SAID, "LET US MAKE
MAN IN OUR IMAGE, AFTER
OUR LIKENESS."

GENESIS 1:26

IDENTIFY YOUR ROOTS

We will spend this first week in Lent reflecting on the foundation of the human heart—the love of God. God is love. We hear it so often that it can begin to lose its fervor. But it doesn't matter whether human fervor accompanies the statement or not, because this truth isn't contingent on the emotions those three words can or can't elicit. Here is the fact of the matter: Who God is says a lot about who I am and who you are. So if God is love, what does that mean about you, and the hidden center of your being, your heart? (See *CCC*, 2563.) In his Wednesday Audience on December 6, 1978, St. John Paul II described the words of Genesis 1:26, "Let us make man in our image, after our likeness," as an indicator that God drew man from God's own being.

I once met a priest who seemed destined to be a saint. At one point in this priest's life, St. Padre Pio had been his confessor. He had also served as a retreat director for St. Teresa of Calcutta, so I decided that I wanted him to hear my confession. I wanted this friend of the saints to share what he had received with me. At the end of my confession, he asked if I believe that when God the Father looks at me, he sees Jesus. At first I thought this might be heresy, but then I remembered 2 Corinthians 3:18, "We all are being changed into his likeness from one degree of glory to another." That has never left me.

To no credit of our own, but through the merits of our Lord Jesus Christ, when God the Father looks at each of us, he sees Jesus. He not only sees Jesus but also his own life, his own image, which we cannot disfigure. While we hold the power to distort the likeness, the image of God is impressed upon us whether we recognize it or not. (That is a theology lesson for another day.) This image that we bear—we cannot ruin it, we cannot shake it, we cannot depart from it, thanks be to God. The love between God the Father and God the Son is so profound that the uncreated fruit of their love is the Holy Spirit. You and I were conceived in and through this dynamism of love. We are the fruit of it, and we are marked by it to our core. It is the root that holds us in existence: God's love.

REFLECT

1. Have you ever thought of yourself as created fruit of God's love, as being conceived within and by God's love? For your prayer today, imagine yourself abiding in the love of the Trinity—the dynamism of love between the Father, the Son, and the uncreated fruit, the Holy Spirit. Place yourself in conversation with the three persons of the Trinity as the created fruit of their love.
2. What are signs you see in yourself that you are created fruit of God's love?

_____

_____

_____

_____

_____

_____

_____

_____

_____

PRAY

*ALMIGHTY GOD, YOU CREATED EACH
OF US WITH A FATHER'S ATTENTIVE
AND INTIMATE CARE. HELP ME TO
RECEIVE YOUR LOVING GAZE, TO SIT
FIRMLY IN THE REALITY THAT I AM
YOUR BELOVED CHILD. ABIDE WITH
ME THIS DAY, AND WELCOME ME
INTO THE LOVE YOU SHARE WITH THE
SPIRIT AND YOUR SON. AMEN.*

FIRST WEEK OF LENT

MONDAY

I ASSURE YOU, WE ARE BATHED IN LOVE
AND MERCY. WE EACH HAVE A FATHER,
A BROTHER, A FRIEND, A SPOUSE OF
OUR SOUL, KING OF OUR HEARTS,
REDEEMER AND SAVIOR; BENT DOWN
OVER US, OVER OUR WEAKNESS, AND
OUR IMPOTENCE LIKE THAT OF LITTLE
CHILDREN; WITH AN INEXPRESSIBLE
GENTLENESS. . . . A JESUS HAUNTED BY
THE DESIRE TO SAVE US BY ALL MEANS,
WHO HAS OPENED HEAVEN UNDER OUR
FEET; AND WE LIVE TOO OFTEN LIKE
ORPHANS, LIKE ABANDONED CHILDREN
AS IF IT WERE HELL WHICH HAD BEEN
OPENED UNDER OUR FEET. WE ARE MEN
OF LITTLE FAITH.

JEAN DU COEUR DE JÉSUS D'ELBÉE,
I BELIEVE IN LOVE: A PERSONAL RETREAT
BASED ON THE TEACHING OF
ST. THÉRÈSE OF LISIEUX

BELIEVE IN LOVE

One evening during a video-conference class for novices, we were studying the Gospel of John, and as we were working our way through chapter 6, I was suddenly overcome with emotion. Our professor, a deacon in the Melkite rite, read the words in John 6:21: "They were glad to take him into the boat." It's easy to gloss over this simple statement, but when we look again, there's something striking about the genuine and simple gladness the disciples felt as they realized Christ was with them. That touched me deeply and infused me with a deep awareness of the intimate relationship between Jesus and his disciples. Later on in the chapter, Jesus tells them, "He who believes has eternal life" (Jn 6:47). And then, once Jesus reveals to the crowd that our salvation will come through consuming his flesh and blood, many reject his gift of self, refusing to believe in this kind of love.

In further vulnerability, Jesus turns to the remaining disciples and asks them if they, too, will leave, to which Peter responds, "We have believed" (Jn 6:69). I sat weeping that night during what was supposed to be an academic class. The great gift and treasure of the faith to believe was impressed upon me, *and* I realized that Jesus's own heart is moved by our belief in him; it is indeed the invitation that he awaits.

Belief was not the disciples' own work, but rather a grace or gift given to them by God that they were stewarding well. In John 6:21, they are in the midst of a storm with high winds, and they are glad. In verse 69, they are in the minority, sure to look like fools or be perceived as crazy, and yet they do not waver in their belief. The reason our belief and not our individual works warrants eternal life is because being receptive and open to the graces to believe is far more intimate than performing the external actions that give the appearance of belief. He who believes has allowed God to enter in and govern, come what may, whether storms or loneliness. If you picked up this journal, you are to some degree expressing belief. This gift is one we must never cease to beg the Lord to increase in us, so that we can proclaim from ever greater depths of our hearts, through the power of his reign in us: "I have come to believe in and know love."

REFLECT

1. Identify an area of your life where you struggle or suffer such that it impacts your ability to believe in God's love. Imagine that experience is a particular untended area of the wilderness of your heart, and then intentionally invite Jesus there. Breathe deeply a few times, opening up your rib cage with each breath, inviting Jesus into that area of your heart.
2. Turn over control of that area to him, asking for the grace to be glad at his coming. If you do not know of an area where you could grow in belief in God's love, pray today for the graces to have your eyes opened. If you have time, journal about this experience.

PRAY

JESUS OUR BROTHER, YOU COME TO BRING US THE FULLNESS OF GOD'S LOVE, AND YOU WALK WITH US IN EVERY MOMENT OF OUR LIVES. I TURN MYSELF OVER TO YOU TODAY, READY TO RECEIVE WHAT YOU HAVE TO OFFER ME, WHICH IS NOTHING LESS THAN YOUR VERY LIFE. HELP ME TRUST THAT YOU ARE SEEKING ME OUT AND WANT TO BRING ME TO THE FATHER. AMEN.

FIRST WEEK OF LENT

TUESDAY

CREATION IS GOD'S FREE
COMMUNICATION OF LOVE,
A COMMUNICATION WHICH,
OUT OF NOTHING, BRINGS
EVERYTHING INTO BEING.
THERE IS NOTHING CREATED
THAT IS NOT FILLED WITH THE
CEASELESS EXCHANGE OF LOVE
THAT MARKS THE INNERMOST
LIFE OF THE TRINITY.

ST. JOHN PAUL II, *ECCLESIA IN ASIA*

PERCEIVE GOD'S LOVE

One day I was sitting with a teen client who was experiencing dissociation—psychological disconnection from her body and the present reality. I finally said, "Okay, we need to go for a walk!" I sensed that she simply needed to *be*—to touch grass and smell air. So, we walked ten minutes away from my office into a neighborhood and then turned around and came back the same distance. We talked about her recent experiences that were driving the dissociation, about how being outside can help with dissociation because nature has the ability to ground us in reality. She was a bit anxious in the beginning (and a very fast walker—she is taller than I am, and I told her it had to look like a habited hobbit was chasing a giraffe down the road!).

Eventually she settled back into herself, sharing her awareness of how she felt in the present moment. Then, shortly after we turned to go back the direction from which we had just come, she said very casually, "Oh, look, blackberries!" She had managed to see (while walking) just a few very small blackberries blooming beneath a bunch of greenery. We paused, amazed (because it was summer in Texas), and peered closely at the few blackberries growing there—something we had not seen when we first passed the bush moments before. She was now grounded and could perceive things in the world around her. She could delight in them and experience them as gift.

I have heard that perceiving God's presence is not like playing hide-and-seek for a small object hidden within a vast space. Rather, perceiving God's presence is more appropriately likened to being in water and perceiving the reality of the water: we are submerged in God's presence, and if God is love, then we are submerged in love. We just need to slow down, settle back into ourselves, and perceive it—just as that young woman was able to spot blackberries miraculously growing in the Texas heat.

Today, slow down and settle a bit more into yourself, especially when fulfilling your Lenten practices, and perceive God's love around you—in the people and the world he has created. Perceive the love you constantly abide in.

REFLECT

1. Sometime today, either go for a walk (if you are able) or sit quietly outside in nature for a period of time in silence (no cell phone, no headphones or earbuds), and take in all that is around you as "God's free communication of love."
2. Pray with Psalm 104. What does this psalm remind you of, and why do you think it would have been important for the psalmist to remind himself of these works of God?

_____

_____

_____

_____

_____

_____

_____

_____

_____

PRAY

*GOD OUR CREATOR, YOUR LOVE
HOLDS US IN BEING—THERE IS
NOWHERE YOU WON'T GO TO BE
WITH US. SUSTAIN ME WITH YOUR
ABIDING PRESENCE, AND HELP ME
PERCEIVE YOUR CLOSENESS. LET ME
HEAR YOUR VOICE THROUGH ALL THE
STILLNESS AND NOISE OF MY LIFE.
AMEN.*

FIRST WEEK OF LENT

WEDNESDAY

JOY IS THE FRUIT OF FAITH. IT
IS BEING AWARE OF [GOD'S]
PRESENCE AND FRIENDSHIP
EVERY DAY.

**POPE BENEDICT XVI, MESSAGE FOR
THE 27TH WORLD YOUTH DAY, 2012**

ABIDE IN JOY

Every New Year's Eve, the Sisters in my community spend extended time in Adoration before the Blessed Sacrament, ringing in the New Year by adoring Jesus on the altar. Several years ago I began to spend those hours in the evening with Jesus looking back over the year, asking the Lord what he wanted me to remember or focus on in the year ahead. I have always perceived a clear message from the Lord in those last hours of the year.

One year, the message I perceived in my mind and heart was, "Take me with you." See, I was busy with all *my* things and *my* activities and *my* ministries. I would check in with Jesus in the morning, when returning home to the convent in the afternoon, and maybe during the day for routine prayers and when I needed something, but I didn't really take him with me. I didn't really share life with him throughout the day.

How many of us do that? Do we have intimate conversations with Jesus only for special reasons? How often, when something wonderful is happening, do we pause and pray quietly to ourselves, "Jesus, what do you think about all this?" Or, "Jesus, thank you for sharing in this joy with me, for your presence and your friendship"? As religious sisters, we call ourselves spouses of Christ, and I was struck that New Year's Eve to be told that my spouse just wanted to come along with me, to be remembered beyond the corners and pockets of time I had tucked him into.

Sometimes people will say Jesus is a gentleman, and I get it. I know what they are trying to say, but this is not my favorite saying. Christ did not, after offering his life on Good Friday, descend into the depths of hell on Holy Saturday and then ascend to the heights of heaven at the Ascension to be a gentleman. He did that so his presence could literally soak through every speck of our lives. He doesn't want to be a quiet gentleman knocking on the door as a potential guest—he wants to *reign*. He wants our hearts to be his home, his abode, his residence, his dwelling. Jesus wants to hold and keep all that occurs in your heart, and that includes your joys!

REFLECT

1. Spend time contemplating a recent joyful memory or perhaps one of the most joyful memories you have. Walk through the memory from beginning to end, as though watching it like a movie or revisiting it with Jesus.
2. Ask God for the grace to know his presence more deeply in this moment and in all the moments of your life, and offer your gratitude.

_____

_____

_____

_____

_____

_____

_____

_____

_____

_____

PRAY

_LORD JESUS, YOU CAME TO RULE
THE EARTH WITH THE FATHER'S ALL-
CONSUMING LOVE. EVEN NOW, YOU
STAND READY TO BREAK INTO MY LIFE
AND TRANSFORM MY HEART. HELP ME
TO TURN MY LIFE OVER TO YOU AND
TO WELCOME YOUR PRESENCE WITH
ME IN EVERY MOMENT. AMEN._

FIRST WEEK OF LENT

THURSDAY

I AM WITH YOU ALWAYS.

MATTHEW 28:20

ABIDE ALWAYS

I wonder if St. Paul knew the debacle that would ensue centuries later when he wrote the words of Ephesians 5:22, "Wives, be subject to your husbands." So many of us have such strong reactions to those words that it causes us to miss the amazing words that come just a few verses later: "Even so husbands should love their wives as their own bodies. He who loves his wife loves himself. For no man ever hates his own flesh, but nourishes it and cherishes it, *as Christ does the Church*" (Eph 5:28–29, emphasis added). Yes, above all, Ephesians is about *the* bridegroom Christ and *the* bride, his Church—you and me. Not only that, but it refers to the fact that our flesh (by virtue of our baptism) has been wedded to Christ's flesh, so that he loves it as his own.

Christ cannot help but abide with and in you, because you are intimately and intricately connected to him; this is why, as I shared before, when the Father looks at you, he sees Jesus. Your heart is his very own self. But what about the other direction? If Christ looks at you so intimately that he sees you as his own flesh, then what does that mean for our view of God? How we see God, then, impacts how we see ourselves, and not just a little bit, but to the core—or rather, *cor*, the Latin word for "heart."

I met a psychologist once whose key area of study was the impact of problematic God images on mental-health healing. He recognized in his work that problematic views of God that were implicit to the client (meaning beneath the surface and not something the client was consciously aware of) could have negative impacts on the healing process. He developed an instrument called the IRiS, Implicit Religion Incomplete Sentences, inviting clients to complete sentences about their faith as spontaneously as possible, and then look back at those sentences and see if there are some implicit concerns that were made explicit through the activity. I want to invite you today into this same exercise, which you'll find in the appendix of this journal.

If we are going to understand that our hearts are created in, permeated with, and the home of love, we have to improve our view of God, who is Love. For he abides with us always, not out of pity, but because he cannot help himself.

REFLECT

Complete the Implicit Religion Incomplete Sentences activity provided in the appendix. You will need your own journal to write the answers for the activity in. If you like, you can use the lines below to reflect on the activity.

_____

_____

_____

_____

_____

_____

_____

_____

PRAY

*LOVING GOD, IN YOUR GOODNESS
YOU ALLOW US TO KNOW YOU, AND
AT THE SAME TIME YOU ARE A GREAT
MYSTERY. HELP ME TO CLING TO
KNOWLEDGE OF YOU THAT IS TRUE,
GOOD, AND BEAUTIFUL AND TO
SURRENDER THE IDEAS I HAVE ABOUT
YOU THAT ARE NOT TRUE AND NOT
HELPFUL. AMEN.*

FIRST WEEK OF LENT

FRIDAY

TEACHER, DO YOU NOT CARE IF
WE PERISH?

MARK 4:38

ABIDE IN SUFFERING
AND SORROW

The first time I realized the closeness of Jesus during times of suffering, my instinctive reaction was one of irritation. I thought, *If you're so close and you're God, why did I even have to suffer?* I have grown past that, but I share it with you now so that if it is your experience, you know you're not alone. I had to realize that Christ never promises us that his presence will remove the reality of suffering; in fact, he promises that we *will* have trouble in the world (see John 16:33).

During the COVID pandemic, Pope Francis gave an extraordinary *urbi et orbi* blessing (to the city and to the whole world), and I was captivated. This elderly man slowly walked out into a strikingly empty St. Peter's Square, needing assistance up and down the stairs. I was captivated by his frailty, by the dark, rainy sky, and by the brilliance of his white cassock against the dark sky. I was captivated by the faith; if it were not true, then the only other thing it could have been was absurd. Pope Francis preached on the disciples in the storm from the fourth chapter of Mark's gospel—their frustration with a sleeping Jesus, and their willingness to cry out to him for help.

Pope Francis described our capacity for and dependency on storms and suffering to remind us that we are creatures in desperate need of a savior. Then, the Blessed Sacrament was placed on a temporary altar in the entrance of St. Peter's Basilica. After a time of Adoration, this physically feeble man, strong in faith, lifted Jesus from the altar in the monstrance and blessed the city, and the entire world, which before him was cast in darkness. Why was I captivated? Because Jesus was with us. The world was an absolute mess. I am certain you had some share in that mess in one way or another. In this extraordinary moment of blessing, a man who could not even make it up and down stairs on his own dared to bless the world with the sacramental presence of the Lord. He showed us our Lord asleep in the stern of the boat, reminding us he is indeed still in our boat and has not abandoned us. He abides most profoundly in our need for him, in our sorrow. Pope Francis dared us to wake the Lord and cast all our anxieties on him, for he cares for us (see 1 Peter 5:7).

REFLECT

Similar to this past Wednesday, recall a time of deep suffering in your life and look back at it with Jesus to see where he was in all of it and what he was doing. I encourage you to place a crucifix in your hands for this prayer, or place yourself in front of an image of a crucifix or a crucifix on a wall. Once you finish the review of the experience with Jesus, speak to him as you would a friend. Share with Jesus what you noticed as you reviewed the time of suffering.

_____

_____

_____

_____

_____

_____

_____

_____

PRAY

*JESUS, OUR SAVIOR, YOU CAME TO
SHARE LIFE WITH US, TO STAND WITH
US IN OUR JOYS AND SORROWS.
WE KNOW OUR WORLD IS FULL
OF TROUBLE—WE SEE IT IN OUR
OWN LIVES—YET THAT DOES NOT
STOP YOU FROM APPROACHING US.
ABIDE WITH ME, ESPECIALLY IN MY
SUFFERING, AND TEACH ME TO LEAN
ON YOU, FOR YOU CAME TO HOLD US
CLOSE. AMEN.*

FIRST WEEK OF LENT

SATURDAY

BY BAPTISM WE ARE MADE FLESH
OF THE CRUCIFIED.

POPE ST. LEO THE GREAT

REVERENCE THE WATERS

If you're using this journal for Lent, it's likely that you've been baptized or are at least hoping to be baptized soon. I visited a parish several years ago and heard a priest speak of the waters of baptism in a unique and powerful way. He said that we are placed in the waters at our baptism and that it is our work over the course of our lives to become deep-sea divers in these waters, sinking more deeply and more profoundly into the identify conferred on us through the waters—the identity as children of God, indelibly marked as such. Our church fathers referred to the baptismal font as the womb of the Church. In it, we are each born into our identity as children of God, and throughout our lives we sink more deeply down into this identity; we grow into it.

This week we looked at the roots of our hearts, the sources from which our hearts grow. Next week, we will look at what that growth tends toward. For today's reverence day—to bridge the gap between the root and the end toward which the journey and process of growth tend—I would like to place you back into your baptismal waters.

My favorite flower is the water lily. I love to kayak, and it's only from a kayak that I ever have a chance to admire my favorite flower up close. The water lily is only as beautiful as it is because its roots run so deep beneath the surface of the water. Its beauty is also connected to its determined upward growth toward the light, toward the sun.

These Saturdays are opportunities to sink more deeply into Christ's love and his impact on us during these Lenten days. They are opportunities to spend some time integrating our experience during the week of being deeply rooted in the Love that created us and sustains us—despite our waywardness on the journey— with our ongoing upward growth toward God's hopes for us. They are opportunities to dive more deeply into the great mystery and gift of the waters of our baptism and the good work those waters began and sustain in us. Water is essential to the formation and nourishment of the wilderness. It cleanses, washes, corrodes, and chips away. Allow yourself today to sink more deeply into what is at work in you during these last few days.

REFLECT

1. Place yourself in the presence of God, and take on a spirit of receptivity. How has life been for you this week: ordinary or exceptional, messy or tidy, connected or disconnected?

2. How are you feeling about the presence of God in relationships: with yourself, others, and God? Choose one experience that stands out, and reflect:

   ✢ How does this experience remind me of other events in my life?

   ✢ Is there a scripture or maxim (saying) that seems to fit this experience?

   ✢ Is there a pattern or theme in my life that this event relates to?

   ✢ How am I feeling now as I remember it?

3. Listen to the movement within your heart:

   ✢ What is moving now as I reflect on this event?

   ✢ Am I being drawn to something deeper, perhaps gratitude or an action?

   ✢ In general, what is going on inside of me?

_____

_____

_____

_____

_____

_____

_____

_____

_____

PRAY

*JESUS, YOU ARE LIFE-GIVING
WATER. YOU COME TO CLEANSE
US AND RESTORE US AND GIVE US
STRENGTH. HELP ME SUBMERGE
MYSELF INTO YOUR LOVE. WASH
AWAY MY SELFISHNESS AND SMALL-
MINDEDNESS AND STUBBORNNESS,
AND HELP ME DRINK IN YOUR
PRESENCE HERE WITH ME. AMEN.*

SECOND WEEK
OF LENT

A HEART MADE FOR RELATIONSHIP

SECOND WEEK OF LENT

SUNDAY

I AM NOT ALONE.

JOHN 16:32

IMAGE YOUR CREATOR

I've been told that I have my father's personality and that I look like my mother. As my niece has grown, it's been shocking to see the similarities in our personalities. We *know* that we share traits with our family members, but to see it incarnate is a whole other matter. Last week we touched on being made in God's image, and if this is so, then as is the case with family, we share traits with our Father, God.

St. John Paul II, in his Wednesday audiences called the *Theology of the Body*, gave us a profound insight into what it means to image, or mirror, God. We know that God is a communion of three distinct persons. We learn throughout the *Theology of the Body* that part of the way we image God is that we, like God, make sense only in the context of relationship. We see this in the book of Genesis; Adam knows he is not like the animals, but he does not declare a knowledge of what he is until he is placed in relationship with Eve, with another human. In this relationship he is able to know himself. This is revealed to us in the Church document *Gaudium et Spes*, where we read the words "Man cannot fully find himself except through a sincere gift of himself" (24).

In other words, we cannot comprehend our existence apart from relationship, because it is what we were made for. We bear this image of communion. Today, I invite you to spend time with Jesus's priestly prayer in John's gospel (chapters 14 through 16), keeping your eye open for themes of relationship. Jesus longs for us to have what he has with the Father because he knows this will make our joy full and complete.

In the Gospel of John, during Jesus's priestly prayer, right before he turns the direction of his words away from the disciples and to the Father, Jesus tells the disciples that even when they leave him alone, he is still not alone, because the Father is with him (see John 16:32). In a sense, when Jesus enters into our hearts this priestly prayer echoes, calling us into relationship with one another, for one another, and ultimately with Jesus, so he can give us what he has with the Father, the very thing we were created for.

REFLECT

1. Pray with chapters 14–16 in the Gospel of John, and notice phrases or words that stand out to you.
2. Reflect on areas of your life where you may be feeling lonely. Invite Jesus into those places in your heart, and let his words repeat in your prayer, "I am not alone."
3. If you would like to go a step further, pray also with the first Mass reading for today (Gn 15:5–12, 17–18). Notice God's desire for covenantal relationship with Abraham, the smoke passing through his offering.

PRAY

*HEAVENLY FATHER, YOUR IMAGE
IS IMPRESSED UPON MY HEART.
EVERYWHERE I GO, YOU ARE WITH ME.
HELP ME TO REMEMBER THAT I AM
NEVER ALONE. AMEN.*

SECOND WEEK OF LENT

MONDAY

I UNDERSTOOD THAT THE CHURCH
HAS A HEART, AND THAT THIS HEART
BURNS WITH LOVE. I UNDERSTOOD
THAT LOVE ALONE MAKES ITS MEMBERS
ACT, THAT IF THIS LOVE WERE TO
BE EXTINGUISHED, THE APOSTLES
WOULD NO LONGER PREACH THE
GOSPEL, THE MARTYRS WOULD
REFUSE TO SHED THEIR BLOOD. . . .
I UNDERSTOOD THAT LOVE IS ALL
THINGS, THAT IT EMBRACES ALL TIMES
AND ALL PLACES.

ST. THÉRÈSE OF LISIEUX,
THE STORY OF A SOUL

FERTILIZE THE SOIL

One week I found myself dealing with escalating pain in one of my bottom teeth, so I made a dentist appointment. The dentist looked at the area of complaint and couldn't find anything concerning. He saw something odd on the scans, mentioned a possible biopsy, and referred me to an oral surgeon. The oral surgeon also looked closely at the area of complaint (it was near where I had a previous root canal) but could not find an explanation for my pain. He sent me to a root-canal specialist.

The root-canal specialist listened to me and mentioned something very interesting. He said the nerves in our mouths are like the nerves of our heart. When your heart is hurting, the pain is often referred to other areas of the body—your shoulder, back, or belly. This is because the heart nerves are far reaching. He asked my permission to examine other areas of my mouth with X-rays. Less than three minutes later we discovered a large cavity underneath a filling of one of my *top*-row teeth!

I am prone to cavities because my teeth are so close together. We laughed, and he said, "Let's fix that and see if your pain goes away," and of course, it did. The first dentist could have helped me, but he forgot about the heart-like nerves in the mouth. The reason the nerves of the heart are far reaching to other areas of the body is because it is the heart that gives life to everything else.

St. Thérèse spoke of this in reference to the heart of the Church as love. Without love alive in the heart of the Church, apostles would not preach, martyrs would not shed their blood, men would not become priests, women would not make religious vows, and the list could go on. We would be dead. Here is the thing; you and I do not have relationships—we actually *are* relationships. Bishop Robert Barron wrote in *Catholicism* that it is more proper for us to say we *are* a relationship with God, rather than saying we *have* a relationship with God. Our very existence shares this reality. Each breath we take requires relationship with God. The seat from which this truth radiates is the throne of your heart, and when something is hurting there, in the foundational relationship with God, it refers pain elsewhere.

REFLECT

1. Spend some time today reflecting on a difficult relationship in your life. What might need to be reordered in your foundational relationship with God to improve your experience or view of that difficult relationship?
2. How has pain been referred into your experience of that relationship from your heart, from the place where God sustains you in relationship?

PRAY

*LORD, YOU ARE MY MAKER, AND
WITHOUT YOU, I WOULD NOT EVEN
EXIST. THANK YOU FOR SUSTAINING
ME WITH YOUR LOVE AND FOR THE
GIFT OF YOUR TRUTH. GIVE ME THE
EYES AND HUMILITY TO SEE WHERE
MY HEART NEEDS TENDING. AMEN.*

SECOND WEEK OF LENT

TUESDAY

A FAITHFUL FRIEND IS A STURDY
SHELTER: HE THAT HAS FOUND
ONE HAS FOUND A TREASURE.
THERE IS NOTHING SO PRECIOUS
AS A FAITHFUL FRIEND, AND
NO SCALES CAN MEASURE
HIS EXCELLENCE. A FAITHFUL
FRIEND IS AN ELIXIR OF LIFE.

SIRACH 6:14–16

DELIGHT IN THE FRUIT

Recently a friend of mine made a really tough decision to leave a school community that she thought she would be in until all of her kids graduated from high school. She had experienced many disappointments and conflicts she would have never imagined. As I looked on and tried to have her back throughout it all, what would often dawn on me was that we had to laugh and shout about it, as honestly the only other option would have been to cry.

Something pierces us when we wrap aspects of our life such as education and work into our faith life, and it all goes sideways; the school community she was leaving was a faith-based one. What did we do? We built a fire, and we burned all the things she could find that represented the pain and disappointment. We laughed, we were silly, and we let it go, and if I am being honest, her good example was an opportunity for me to metaphorically toss some of my own mess into the fire that it was time to let go of. This is the power of a good friendship. Yes, good friendships ultimately ought to call us to greater virtue. In good friendships we ought to learn to love God better together.

Also, good friendships are like an elixir of life, as the prophet Sirach says. This elixir can lighten the dark moments, can shine light into our hearts, can build a fire and find joy instead of keeping us in the loss, darkness, disappointment, and pain.

Life can be busy, and we can forget to do simple things such as thank the people who fill our lives with joy and love. We can miss the profound reality that the life and light and joy we receive from them is a share or a reflection of who God is for us. How precious, indeed, is such a treasure.

REFLECT

1. Spend some time today reflecting on a life-giving relationship in your life. What have you learned about who God is in that relationship and also about who you are?
2. If you feel called, speak with or write to that person, and let them know some specific ways that he or she has been a gift to you.

_____

_____

_____

_____

_____

_____

_____

_____

_____

_____

PRAY

*SWEET JESUS, YOU HAVE SEARCHED
ME AND KNOW ME. YOU HAVE PUT
PEOPLE INTO MY LIFE TO SHOW ME
YOUR LOVE. HELP ME TO RECOGNIZE
MY FRIENDS FOR THE GIFT THAT THEY
ARE AND TO BE A GOOD FRIEND IN
RETURN. AMEN.*

SECOND WEEK OF LENT

WEDNESDAY

HE THAT HAS FOUND ONE HAS
FOUND A TREASURE.

SIRACH 6:14

BE REFINED BY THE FIRE

Yes, that is the same verse from Sirach from yesterday about faithful friends. And yes, I am going to assert that difficult relationships are also a treasure; hear me out. When I entered the convent, lo and behold, I did not find contained therein a bunch of angels who walked around giving one another the sign of peace all day. I instead found very human women who, like myself, were works in progress concerning the journey to holiness. And, along the way, as we lived together, we tripped over ourselves and our character defects from time to time.

I struggled frequently with one particular Sister. We would say sarcastic and mean things to each other, and one day this pattern culminated in her telling me that perhaps we should not speak any longer, to which I responded that in my opinion the idea was inspired! We went a few days with this planned silence, and then one day, we both approached a shelf at the same time. She had some physical disabilities, so it was clear that I needed to help her, and God had placed me there to do so. I reached up and handed her the object I knew she wanted without needing her to say, because I had lived with her and had come to know her, so I didn't need her to tell me what she needed from the shelf.

To break our silence, she uttered two words: "Thank you." I responded, "You're welcome." To this day, we have not argued like we did in the past again, and to this day, she is one of the most treasured relationships I have found in religious life, because with her I was able to see the true state of my heart and where exactly Jesus's gaze was fixed in his journey into the wilderness of my heart—what most desperately needed his rescuing touch. How, then, could I not be indebted to this Sister?

Refining fire is painful, of course. It burns, but its end is to refine. Practically speaking, a refiner's fire is a fire used to purify precious materials. In the refining fire, impurities are cleansed and burned away. Can we thank God for our difficult relationships (I am not referring to abusive ones) and lean into what the refiner is seeking to do with the precious material of our heart?

REFLECT

1. Return in prayer to the same difficult relationship you reflected on two days ago, and now answer this additional question: How might God be inviting you to experience purification in that relationship?
2. Close your time in prayer with a slow reading of Exodus 3:2.

_____

_____

_____

_____

_____

_____

_____

_____

_____

_____

PRAY

JESUS, YOU CAME TO RESCUE ME AND TO BE A GUIDE THROUGH THE WILDERNESS OF MY HEART. LIGHT THE WAY FOR ME AS I WADE INTO THESE SHADOWY PLACES. SET MY WHOLE HEART ABLAZE WITH YOUR REFINING FIRE. AMEN.

SECOND WEEK OF LENT

THURSDAY

OVER ALL THESE PUT
ON LOVE, WHICH BINDS
EVERYTHING TOGETHER IN
PERFECT HARMONY.

COLOSSIANS 3:14

STEWARD THE TREASURE

If all relationships—those that are a source of consolation as well as those that act like the refiner's fire on our hearts and souls—are a treasure, then we must steward the treasure well. We can easily overprivatize virtue and holiness, but the fact is, no saint was ever made a saint apart from relationships. Holiness and virtue are relational matters, and virtue is only made visible in the world through a relational act—be it directed toward God or another person.

I have seen this repeatedly with parents I have counseled. (Usually, Dad holds this view, but sometimes Mom does too.) They will look at me side-eyed and reserved, uncertain what all this mental-health stuff could possibly have to do with their child being a disciple of Jesus and a saint. Here is the thing: I can pray a million Rosaries, raise the perfect altar server, and memorize all my prayers in English *and* Latin, but if I never learn to sincerely apologize, to face uncomfortable conversations with virtue, to forgive, to be forgiven, to see conflict as something to move toward versus something to avoid at the cost of my own integrity, and to set boundaries because they are loving, pastoral, and communicate others' and my own dignity, then I will still be miles off the path to holiness and far from bringing Jesus to others.

I have to be honest. I have never been afraid of conflict. I was one of those people who had to learn to lay off the conflict gas pedal; I know this is not the case for everyone. Whether you need to give it a little gas or dial it back a notch, conflict approached well can, in my personal experience, increase relational closeness and intimacy; it does not diminish it. Conflict can be a means to connection, and remember, that is what we were made for: loving relationships.

Our problem with conflict is sometimes twofold. One issue is how we tend to approach conflict with a strategy focused on control rather than connection. Yet, seeking connection in relationships will always take us closer to what our hearts truly long for than seeking control in relationships will. Once we have surrendered the need to be in control, when we face the vulnerabilities that often come with conflict, the second issue we run into is that no one has taught us the skills to deal with conflict! That is going to change today. Please see the Conflict and Connection handout available at www.avemariapress.com/private/page/ wilderness-within-resources for advice on dealing with conflict.

REFLECT

1. Read and pray with Colossians 3:5–17.
2. Reflect on a present relationship in your life or a past relationship that could be approached differently by viewing conflict from the perspective of one who is seeking to be a good steward of a treasured relationship.

_____

_____

_____

_____

_____

_____

_____

_____

PRAY

_LORD, YOU HAVE MADE US FOR
RELATIONSHIP, AND I DO NOT
EXIST IN A VACUUM. HELP ME
TO UNDERSTAND MY CURRENT
APPROACH TO CONFLICT AND
TO SEE HOW CONFLICT CAN BE A
MEANS FOR CONNECTION. GIVE
ME THE COURAGE TO FACE MY
VULNERABILITIES AND TO HONOR
YOU IN HOW I LOVE OTHERS. AMEN._

SECOND WEEK OF LENT

FRIDAY

THEREFORE, BEHOLD, I WILL
ALLURE HER, AND BRING HER
INTO THE WILDERNESS AND
SPEAK TENDERLY TO HER.

HOSEA 2:14

EMBRACE THE MYSTERY

I highly recommend the book *Jesus the Bridegroom* by Brant Pitre. In it he helps to bring home the fact that the relationship between God and his Church is one of bridegroom to bride, and salvation history is perhaps one extended proposal, tending toward a wedding banquet. In a sense, our Lord remains on bended knee. When we began our Lenten journey, we reflected on why Jesus enters into the wilderness in the first place. Yes, he enters to restore order and to rescue us. But it does not end there; we are being rescued for a purpose, and that purpose is relationship, a spousal one to be exact. The wilderness is a place of restoration, it is a place of rescue, but it is also a place of invitation back into a renewed spousal relationship with the Lord. The prophet does not mince words when he speaks on behalf of the Lord:

> And in that day, says the LORD, you will call me, "My husband," and no longer will you call me, "My Ba'al." I will remove the names of the Ba'als from her mouth, and they shall be mentioned by name no more. And I will make for you a covenant on that day with the beasts of the field, the birds of the air, and the creeping things of the ground; and I will abolish the bow, the sword, and war from the land; and I will make you lie down in safety. And I will espouse you for ever; I will espouse you in righteousness and in justice, in steadfast love, and in mercy. I will espouse you in faithfulness; and you shall know the LORD. (Hos 2:16–20)

Sound familiar? The place of betrothal to God is like the garden before it became a wilderness due to sin. Our capacity to embrace this spousal mystery will directly impact our ability to see the Cross as more than a reason to feel sorrow for sin or experience tearful sentiments on Good Friday. Entering into this spousal mystery will transform our view of the Cross into a proposal, an invitation to an everlasting and covenantal relationship. In short, this spousal mystery makes the Cross lovely.

Here is the good news. All of our relationships are then opportunities to move toward or away from this primary relational end. They are opportunities to understand the mystery of God's love for us and the inevitable proposal he will make in the wilderness.

REFLECT

Sit quietly today before an image of a crucifix or an actual crucifix (hold one in your hands if you like) for at least five minutes in silence. Behold Christ on the Cross as One who seeks to propose a spousal relationship to you through his Passion.

PRAY

*JESUS, YOU DIED ON THE CROSS
SO THAT WE WOULD HAVE ETERNAL
LIFE WITH YOU. YOUR ACT OF SELF-
GIFT MIRRORS THE DAILY CALL IN
MY LIFE TO RECOGNIZE GOD'S LOVE
PRESENT IN MY RELATIONSHIPS.
HELP ME GIVE OF MYSELF AND TO GO
BRAVELY INTO THE FRIENDSHIPS AND
RELATIONSHIPS YOU HAVE PUT INTO
MY LIFE. AMEN.*

SECOND WEEK OF LENT

SATURDAY

SPEAK TO HIM, THOU, FOR HE
HEARS, AND SPIRIT WITH SPIRIT
CAN MEET—
CLOSER IS HE THAN BREATHING,
AND NEARER THAN HANDS
AND FEET.

**ALFRED LORD TENNYSON,
"THE HIGHER PANTHEISM"**

REVERENCE LOVE

At the dinner celebration after my final vows, my uncle gave a toast. I have since titled it "The Measure of God's Love Toast." What my uncle wanted everyone to understand is that we have a way to quantify God's love. If we took my uncle's advice and followed his means of measuring God's love, we would be amazed. How does my uncle say you can measure God's love? By counting your breaths in a day.

I fear I brushed over it far too casually on Monday—the truth that you *are* a relationship. It would be irreverent of me not to return to it today. What an awesome truth: that our existential foundation is relationship and that the breath you literally just took was by virtue of God relating to you. We are quite literally sustained in his faithful relationship to us, revealed in each breath.

This is a mystery, which means we are *not* supposed to totally get it. This mystery should give us more pause in our relationships to ourselves, others, and especially to God, because we are face-to-face with something we will need a lifetime of help to understand to any significant degree. So much more is at hand in our relationships than we sometimes realize. I heard once that when St. Teresa of Calcutta met a person, she would pause before speaking because she was first greeting Jesus in them. She got it. In his *Confessions*, St. Augustine said that God is "*intimior intimo meo*," more inward than what is inmost in me—or, more simply, nearer to me than I am to myself. This mystery should not frighten us, for it is good news. If we have to choose who will fully get it, God or ourselves, our odds are always better with God. Slow down for this time of integration today, perhaps spending some time in intentional silence. Do not run ahead too quickly without pausing to measure God's love in your breaths.

REFLECT

1. Place yourself in the presence of God, and take on a spirit of receptivity. How has life been for you this week: ordinary or exceptional, messy or tidy, connected or disconnected?

2. How are you feeling about the presence of God in relationships: with yourself, others, and God? Choose one experience that stands out and reflect:

    ✦ How does this experience remind me of other events in my life?

    ✦ Is there a scripture or maxim (saying) that seems to fit this experience?

    ✦ Is there a pattern or theme in my life that this event relates to?

    ✦ How am I feeling now as I remember it?

3. Listen to the movement within your heart:

    ✦ What is moving now as I reflect on this event?

    ✦ Am I being drawn to something deeper, perhaps gratitude or an action?

    ✦ In general, what is going on inside of me?

_____

_____

_____

_____

_____

_____

_____

_____

_____

PRAY

*LORD OF LIFE, YOU ARE NEARER TO
ME THAN I AM TO MYSELF. HELP ME
TO INTERNALIZE THIS TRUTH AND
TO MEASURE YOUR LOVE TODAY.
EVEN WHEN I LACK UNDERSTANDING,
GIVE ME THE GRACE TO BRING LOVE
INTO THE WORLD AND INTO MY
RELATIONSHIPS. I TRUST YOU WITH
EVERYTHING. AMEN.*

THIRD WEEK
OF LENT

A HEART
WOUNDED
BY SIN

THIRD WEEK OF LENT

SUNDAY

I BAPTIZE YOU WITH WATER FOR
REPENTANCE, BUT HE WHO IS
COMING AFTER ME IS MIGHTIER
THAN I, WHOSE SANDALS I AM
NOT WORTHY TO CARRY; HE WILL
BAPTIZE YOU WITH THE HOLY
SPIRIT AND WITH FIRE.

MATTHEW 3:11

OPEN THE DOOR

On the third Sunday of Lent, Catholic parishes that have elect who will be receiving sacraments at the Easter Vigil will often choose to use the Mass readings for what is called year A in the Mass Lectionary. That means the gospel story of the woman at the well is being proclaimed at many parishes today. The woman at the well is one of my favorite stories in the Bible because it is the first time Jesus clearly and openly says that he is the Messiah, and, as we touched on last Friday, this ultimately is the proclamation of a relationship so profound that it is spousal.

At the well with St. Photina, Jesus is clear about his intentions toward us for the first time. St. Photina is seeking water to quench her thirst. In the first reading for today's readings (year A) the Israelites complain of thirst in the wilderness, and God provides the water through Moses's striking the rock. The elect who will be receiving the sacraments at Easter will be born into the Church through water and fire: the waters of the baptismal font and the fire of the Holy Spirit given to them in Confirmation.

Why all this water and fire? In Jewish wedding (or espousal) customs, the bride would wash or cleanse in what was called a mikveh in preparation for the wedding. This was something like a bachelorette party; her friends would gather and bring fine soaps and perfumes and assist her in this preparation.

This week, as we begin to open the door to the wilderness of our hearts, inviting Jesus in, I want us to avoid the self-centered trappings that make these types of reflections dark and burdensome. This is a time to reflect on our sins and our wounds, but ultimately, this is not a time of darkness. It is a time to sip from the cup of life-giving water. This is a time to be purified by fire that does not consume. This is the Messiah entering in, not because he is horrified with the state of your heart, but rather because he sees what and who you truly are, and he wants to give you the opportunity to see as he sees. To see as he sees requires that we be cleansed and purified. Pay far more attention to him than you do to your wounds.

REFLECT

1. Spend time praying with John 4:5–42. Jesus knows St. Photina and her whole story. He sees her. Place yourself in the scene, and have a conversation with Jesus in prayer.
2. What would Jesus say to you about your story with your past and your struggles that others may not know or understand, but he does?

_____

_____

_____

_____

_____

_____

_____

_____

_____

_____

PRAY

*JESUS, OUR LIFE-GIVING MESSIAH,
YOU ARE WAITING TO MEET US
IN THE DEEPEST WELLS OF OUR
HEARTS, READY TO BRING US THE
REFRESHING AND CLEANSING WATER
OF YOUR LOVE. YOU KNOW MY
DEEPEST LONGINGS AND MY DEEPEST
WOUNDS, AND YOU ARE THE ONLY
PLACE WHERE I CAN FIND PEACE
AND REST. GIVE ME COURAGE TO
RESPOND TO YOUR CLOSENESS.
AMEN.*

83

THIRD WEEK OF LENT

MONDAY

IF WE LOOK ONLY AT OURSELVES,
WITH OUR OWN LIMITATIONS
AND SINS, WE QUICKLY
GIVE WAY TO SADNESS AND
DISCOURAGEMENT. BUT IF WE
KEEP OUR EYES FIXED ON THE
LORD, THEN OUR HEARTS ARE
FILLED WITH HOPE.

ST. JOHN PAUL II, ADDRESS TO THE
YOUNG PEOPLE OF NEW ORLEANS,
SEPTEMBER 12, 1987

LET US WORK REDEMPTION

Included in the Spiritual Exercises of St. Ignatius is a reflection on the Incarnation from the viewpoint of the Blessed Trinity, from eternity, reflecting on the decision to save us from sin. St. Ignatius directs the retreatant to look at the world with the Blessed Trinity, seeing all that the Father, Son, and Holy Spirit see. We see people all throughout the world, all different and unique, some at peace, some at war, some laughing, some weeping, some well, some ill. The retreatant is encouraged to reflect on what the three divine persons see in how we speak to one another and about one another, including swearing and blaspheming.

What would we add today? Fighting with each other on the internet, saying things about and to one another online that we would not dare speak face-to-face. Ministers leveraging the pain and woundedness of the members of the Body of Christ, becoming false heroes, gods without a cross or a sacrifice in the flesh, gaining profit and positioning themselves as having all the answers and being the heralds of truth. Deep divisions within the Body of Christ as well as even deeper corruption.

In this particular exercise, St. Ignatius writes that in the midst of all of this, the three divine persons respond with the words, "Let us work the redemption of the human race." We are killing one another, swearing against one another, exploiting one another for profit—and the divine persons *move closer*, desiring to help, preparing an outpouring from their own divine life.

The angel Gabriel fulfills his duty as an ambassador and the Blessed Virgin humbly submits, all as we struggle. From time to time in prayer, I have found it very helpful for my own continued conversion to stand with the three divine persons, bent over the world in concern, and strive to see what they see and as they see. I pray for the grace to share their gaze and concern toward my own sinfulness and the collective sinfulness in the world. I think from this perspective we cannot help but to become more acutely aware of our own role in the collective troubles of the world.

REFLECT

1. What do you think the gaze of the three divine persons is fixed on today as God looks upon the world, continuing to say, "Let us work the redemption of the human race"?
2. What does the Holy Trinity's gaze desire to redeem in the world, in your city, in your family, and in the world of your own heart?

PRAY

*HOLY GOD, YOU SHARE WITH US THE
INNER GIFTS OF LOVE THAT MOVE
BETWEEN FATHER, SON, AND SPIRIT
IN ORDER TO TRANSFORM US AND
MAKE US COLLABORATORS IN YOUR
WORK OF REDEMPTION. HELP ME
MOVE CLOSER TO BROKENNESS IN
THE WORLD AND IN MYSELF AND
TO POUR OUT THERE THE LOVE I
RECEIVE FROM YOU. AMEN.*

THIRD WEEK OF LENT

TUESDAY

THE ROOT OF SIN IS IN THE HEART OF
MAN, IN HIS FREE WILL, ACCORDING
TO THE TEACHING OF THE LORD:
"FOR OUT OF THE HEART COME EVIL
THOUGHTS, MURDER, ADULTERY,
FORNICATION, THEFT, FALSE WITNESS,
SLANDER. THESE ARE WHAT DEFILE
A MAN." BUT IN THE HEART ALSO
RESIDES CHARITY, THE SOURCE OF
THE GOOD AND PURE WORKS, WHICH
SIN WOUNDS.

CATECHISM OF THE CATHOLIC CHURCH,
1853, QUOTING MATTHEW 15:19–20

GO TO THE ROOT

On my very first eight-day silent retreat, my retreat director asked me to reflect on the patterns of sin throughout my life, posing the question to me, "What is the root of your sin?" He asked me to consider the patterns, themes, and common situations surrounding my tendency to sin, and perhaps in those considerations, the root might be revealed. Being an overachiever, I thought my task was to get the answer theologically right: pride. So, the next day I returned with my right answer, the fruit of little prayer, "The root is pride!" My retreat director did not accept the answer and gave me the same assignment again, asking me, "But what is at the root of *your* sin in *your own* words?" That day I did sit down and reflect on the sins I have confessed the longest or most repeatedly throughout my life, how I typically felt before and after, and what my motivations were. What was I seeking with the sin, really seeking? In that prayer I had an answer, and it was not pride. The root of my sin was a strong belief that the best person in my life to count on for the most important things to me was myself.

When I was a postulant we would often help our postulant director with work in the woods behind the convent. One day, Sister spotted a tree that was deeply attached to a vine that was killing it, and she wanted to save the tree. Another postulant and myself tugged with our combined weight and fell to the ground as the vine pulled loose. Our formation director stood over us as we lay on the ground and said in a serious tone, with her Polish accent, "That is what sin does to your soul."

Looking back at our lives and reflecting on the patterns and themes of our sins is not an opportunity to beat ourselves up or to drown in sorrow for our sins. We want to have proper sorrow for our sins, but above all, we want to go to the root, so that, with Jesus's help, our souls can be separated from the poisonous vine of sin. Our goal is to get to the heart of the matter, for it is in the heart where the root of sin lies (see *CCC*, 1853).

REFLECT

1. Journal today about your patterns with sin with the purpose of answering the question, What is the root of your sin?
2. What sins do you find yourself confessing most often, or which have you been confessing for a very long time? What tend to be your feelings before and after the choice to sin? What are the typical circumstances, and what are your motivations?
3. Help Jesus in his efforts in the wilderness to do some clearing and separate old vines from your heart. Today is also a good time to make a plan to go to Confession.

_____

_____

_____

_____

_____

_____

_____

PRAY

MERCIFUL SAVIOR, YOU CAME AMONG US TO HELP US CONFRONT AND OVERCOME SIN. IN CLINGING TO YOU INSTEAD OF OUR SELF-DIRECTED INCLINATIONS, WE FIND FREEDOM AND LIFE. HELP ME TO BE HONEST WITH MYSELF ABOUT WHAT HOLDS ME BACK FROM EMBRACING THE DIVINE LIFE YOU OFFER, AND GIVE ME CONFIDENCE THAT YOU WILL LET NOTHING STAND IN THE WAY OF YOUR MERCIFUL EMBRACE. AMEN.

THIRD WEEK OF LENT

WEDNESDAY

WE SHOULD RECALL THAT NO MAN IS AN ISLAND, ENTIRE OF ITSELF. OUR LIVES ARE INVOLVED WITH ONE ANOTHER, THROUGH INNUMERABLE INTERACTIONS THEY ARE LINKED TOGETHER. NO ONE LIVES ALONE. NO ONE SINS ALONE. NO ONE IS SAVED ALONE. THE LIVES OF OTHERS CONTINUALLY SPILL OVER INTO MINE: IN WHAT I THINK, SAY, DO AND ACHIEVE. AND CONVERSELY, MY LIFE SPILLS OVER INTO THAT OF OTHERS: FOR BETTER AND FOR WORSE.

POPE BENEDICT XVI, *SPE SALVI*, 48

TILL THE SOIL

Another aspect of the Spiritual Exercises of St. Ignatius is spending some days reflecting on sin, with the purpose of having greater insight into the root of our own tendency to sin, the motivation or the misdirected desire. As I began these days of prayer on sin in my life, my director invited me to do something unique: read the daily newspaper as a part of my prayer and reflection on sin. He asked me to read through the paper and see the sins of humanity contained within the pages. It was the summer of 2020, a difficult time in our country, so the reality and fruits of sin in the world were very evident to me as I looked through the paper.

When I was in the novitiate, one of the novice directors who attended our intercommunity novitiate events had spent several years of his priesthood in Guatemala. He told a story about the priests of the indigenous religion there who, although married, remained celibate in their marriage as their priesthood required of them. He shared a story of asking an indigenous priest jokingly during a dinner why he would not take the opportunity to be intimate with his own wife! The indigenous priest responded that this would bring harm to the people and that his own sins would cause the people to suffer and the crops to fail. That evening, after the dinner, a terrible storm came, which negatively impacted the crops. Father said he jokingly asked the indigenous priest about the storm, to which he responded that that must have been the *other* village priest of the indigenous religion! Father concluded the story by saying that our lives are not a private matter.

Sometimes we can live under the illusion that the painful realities in the world do not have much to do with us. Pope Benedict XVI tells us otherwise. Not only do the lives of my family, friends, and people in my chosen circle of like-minded folks spill over into mine, but so do the lives of my enemies, the lives of the people I judge, the lives of people who, if I am being honest, I feel better than or am a little disgusted by. Their lives are literally in mine, and mine is in theirs, for better or for worse, as Pope Benedict XVI wrote in his encyclical on hope. What would the world look like if we had greater sensitivity to the consequences of our sins for others?

REFLECT

1. Consider the sins and the root causes you prayed about yesterday, and today continue to pray about that, asking yourself how your family, friends, loved ones, and community have been impacted by these sins.
2. Remember, Jesus is with you in this space, not to condemn you, but to till the soil in your heart that perhaps has not been well tended and is overgrown.

_____

_____

_____

_____

_____

PRAY

*LOVING GOD, YOU ARE A
COMMUNION OF PERSONS IN THE
BLESSED TRINITY. CREATED IN YOUR
IMAGE, WE, TOO, ARE MADE FOR
COMMUNITY AND RELATIONSHIP.
HELP ME REMEMBER THAT MY LIFE IS
NOT MY OWN, THAT YOU MADE US
FOR ONE ANOTHER, AND THAT EVEN
THE MOST PRIVATE PARTS OF MY LIFE
SHAPE THE WAY I PARTICIPATE IN
YOUR FAMILY OF LOVE. STRENGTHEN
ME TO RECOGNIZE AND ROOT OUT
THE SIN THAT HOLDS ME BACK FROM
LIVING FULLY AS ONE OF YOUR
CHILDREN.*

THIRD WEEK OF LENT

THURSDAY

FOR THOUGH WE LIVE IN THE
WORLD WE ARE NOT CARRYING
ON A WORLDLY WAR, FOR THE
WEAPONS OF OUR WARFARE
ARE NOT WORLDLY BUT HAVE
DIVINE POWER TO DESTROY
STRONGHOLDS. WE DESTROY
ARGUMENTS AND EVERY
PROUD OBSTACLE TO THE
KNOWLEDGE OF GOD, AND TAKE
EVERY THOUGHT CAPTIVE TO
OBEY CHRIST.

2 CORINTHIANS 10:3–5

FIND THE PATTERNS

When I began receiving a type of therapy called EMDR, my Christian counselor referenced a book titled *Understanding the Wounded Heart* by Marcus Warner to give me a Christian view of what happens in EMDR therapy. (Eye Movement Desensitization and Reprocessing is "a structured therapy that encourages the patient to briefly focus on the trauma memory while simultaneously experiencing bilateral stimulation [typically eye movements], which is associated with a reduction in the vividness and emotion associated with the trauma memories" [emdria.org].) In his book, Warner uses the acronym WLVS, pronounced wolves, to explain how the enemy can take control within wounded hearts. WLVS stands for wounds, lies, vows, and strongholds. Warner paints the image of a wound causing soil to be turned over or tilled in your heart.

Turning over soil is not necessarily a bad thing. What is good or bad is which seeds are sown in this freshly turned soil. Are they truth seeds, the seeds of the Holy Spirit? Or are they lie seeds, the seeds of the enemy? If the Spirit is able to plant seeds, then their fruit is the fruit of the Spirit: love, joy, kindness, and ultimately continued trust that God is still good. If the enemy is able to take control of the wound by planting lie seeds, then we try to take control of our lives from God, making vows based on the lies we now believe. Vows usually start with the words "I will": "I will never hurt that way again." "I will never trust again." "I will never be vulnerable again."

And then the *S* is for strongholds. Living out the vow over and over again strengthens belief in the lie and creates a stronghold, a block between you and God, a barrier that keeps you turned away from God's power and reliant on your own. The therapy I received helped me to identify some of my patterns of thinking that were rooted in lies, and then, with God's help, to uproot what the enemy had planted.

We have on average sixty thousand thoughts per day, and research tells us that 80 percent, or forty-eight thousand, of them are negative. Contained within those thought patterns are the lies we have believed and the vows we have committed ourselves to. Later we will cover how ultimately to take our thoughts captive, but before we can take our thoughts captive, we have to learn to tune in to what those thoughts even are, especially if they are the fruit of lies and the recitation of vows. God still stands at the site of the wound, giving us the divine power to destroy strongholds.

REFLECT

1. In the field of mental health, negative thought patterns are called cognitive distortions, and cognitive distortions can be grouped into various types. Using the Handout on Thought Patterns and Distortions found on www.avemariapress.com/private/page/wilderness-within-resources, identify thought distortion patterns that you participate in most often.

2. If possible, identify any vows that may be connected to the thought patterns that most frequently fill your mind. How does identifying the vow help you to better understand your patterns with sin?

PRAY

*GOD OF TRUTH AND LIFE, YOUR
SON COMPARED YOU TO A SOWER
WHO BROADCASTS SEEDS WITH
GENEROSITY. YOU SHARE YOUR
GRACE RECKLESSLY, YET WE OFTEN
HAVE TROUBLE SEEING ALL THE
WAYS YOU PROVIDE FOR US. TURN
THE SOIL IN MY HEART, AND MAKE
MY SOUL FERTILE GROUND FOR THE
GIFTS YOU SHARE. AS I DISCOVER
YOU AT WORK IN MY LIFE, GROW MY
TRUST IN YOUR LOVING CARE.*

THIRD WEEK OF LENT

FRIDAY

SELF-KNOWLEDGE ONLY ENABLES
THE SOUL TO STAND BEFORE GOD IN
TRUTH. YET SELF-KNOWLEDGE OUGHT
NOT BRING ABOUT DISCOURAGEMENT,
PAIN, AND GRIEF, WHICH ARE THE
SURE SIGNS OF PRIDE, CONCEIT AND
EXAGGERATED SELF-SUFFICIENCY:
TO THE CONTRARY, IT OUGHT TO
INSPIRE GREAT PEACE, CONFIDENCE
AND FORTITUDE.

**BL. MARY OF JESUS THE GOOD
SHEPHERD, FOUNDRESS OF THE SISTERS
OF THE HOLY FAMILY OF NAZARETH**

STAND IN TRUTH

I had the honor once of being with a friend who was going to Confession after many years of not having gone. I admired the care he took with his examination of conscience and also that one of the greatest sorrows for his sins was how they might have brought harm to his family. As his appointment with Jesus drew closer, he started to panic! I am embarrassed to admit that I wanted to grab him and say, "Get over yourself!"

The enemy likes to convince us that our sins are far too shameful and awful to utter out loud in a confessional, that the humiliation of it will kill us, that what we have done, and who we think we have become because of it, is somehow outside the reach of God's mercy. In the quote I shared before this meditation, my Mother Foundress takes us by the shoulders, telling us to "get over ourselves" in her guidance that ultimately our pain, grief, dismay, and discouragement in the face of our brokenness and sinfulness is pride, conceit, and exaggerated self-sufficiency! Ouch! Let me put it a little differently: It is as if we say, "What I have done, who I believe I have become, the humiliation and embarrassment I may feel to say these things out loud are more powerful than Jesus on the Cross, than his flesh and blood." When we cower at opportunities to stand before God in truth, we unwittingly undermine the power of the Cross and falsely diminish the breadth and length and height and depth of God's infinite mercy (see Ephesians 3:18).

Continued from the opening quote for today, Mother Foundress goes on to say:

> Once we admit, by grace, our defects, sinfulness,
> and weakness, we shall the sooner and more secure-
> ly attain to God and to a life of virtue. Since virtue
> depends upon the recognition of our helplessness
> and upon humility, it will develop deeper roots and

will thrive more vigorously. Your efforts should tend in that direction, namely, to come to know yourself, doing this as peacefully, hopefully, and simply as a child in relation to its mother. Let not your faults and failures surprise you, do not become indignant over them. Rest assured that the Lord is pleased a thousandfold more by a soul who is susceptible to many falls, but who knowing her weakness, turns to God in humility, than by another who is less prone to fall and is seemingly more perfect, but is self-confident and self-sufficient.

REFLECT

1. Pray before a crucifix today, anywhere you can find one (look one up online if needed).
2. Speak with Jesus as you would with a friend about what has stood out to you in your reflections this week. Relate it all to him in your prayer honestly, as if you are telling him something he does not already know.
3. Ask Jesus for the grace to be hopeful in the face of your self-awareness and abandoned to his mercy, for it is a grace to see yourself in truth and an even greater grace to stand before our crucified Lord in truth.

PRAY

*JESUS, YOU ARE THE LOVE OF THE
FATHER COME TO LIVE AMONG
US. YOU KNOW ME BETTER THAN
I KNOW MYSELF, AND DESPITE MY
INSUFFICIENCY AND WEAKNESSES,
YOU WANT NOTHING MORE THAN TO
GIVE ME ALL OF YOURSELF. GIVE ME
COURAGE TO EMBRACE THE TRUTH
OF MY LIFE THAT IS REVEALED IN THE
LIGHT OF YOUR LOVE AND TO MOVE
WITH CONFIDENT HOPE THAT YOU
WILL HELP ME BECOME MORE LIKE
YOU. AMEN.*

THIRD WEEK OF LENT

SATURDAY

I HAVE FORGOTTEN.

**JESUS TO ST. MARGARET MARY
ALACOQUE**

REVERENCE THE FIRE

Our Sister who serves in vocations ministry is very adventurous. She has a particular activity that she will do for discernment retreats and Confirmation retreats to help the participants understand the nature of God's love. She buys magic flash paper and has the participants write down on the paper any patterns of sin or woundedness that they hope to be freed from; then they nail these pieces of paper to an actual cross. When lit on fire, flash paper vanishes. So, once all of the participants have nailed their burdens to the cross, she lights just one of the papers, and the fire expands so all the sins and burdens and wounds vanish. All that remains is the cross, untouched by the flames. This is what happens with our sins in Confession.

When St. Margaret Mary Alacoque began to have visions of Jesus about the revelation of his Sacred Heart, her confessor, in order to test the validity of her visions, asked her to go back to Jesus and ask him what was the last sin the priest had confessed. Jesus's response to Margaret Mary was "I have forgotten." Confession is like stepping into the burning flame of the Sacred Heart and being not consumed but rather purified.

There is a chance this week may have been difficult in some ways—fire that does not consume can still be hot! This is a necessary process in bringing order to the wilderness: tearing down vines, uprooting weeds, burning the brush. Two things are important. If you have not done so, it is time to make a Confession. Make a plan to go, and know that as I write this, I am praying for you, that you will meet a kind and gentle shepherd in the confessional. Even if for some reason the priest is not who and what you had hoped, it is impossible for the confessional to not be a place of victory.

The second thing that is important is to be mindful about this day of repetition, of reverence. Do not move ahead too hastily. Give yourself the gift of sitting with the blessings of this week. Seeing our sinfulness and brokenness more clearly is likened to sounding the trumpet of Zion, so that the bridegroom (Jesus) leaves his room (see Joel 2:16) to meet his spouse (us, the Church).

REFLECT

1. Place yourself in the presence of God, and take on a spirit of receptivity. How has life been for you this week: ordinary or exceptional, messy or tidy, connected or disconnected?

2. How are you feeling about the presence of God in relationships: with yourself, others, and God? Choose one experience that stands out and reflect:

   ✤ How does this experience remind me of other events in my life?

   ✤ Is there a scripture or maxim (saying) that seems to fit this experience?

   ✤ Is there a pattern or theme in my life that this event relates to?

   ✤ How am I feeling now as I remember it?

3. Listen to the movement within your heart:

   ✤ What is moving now as I reflect on this event?

   ✤ Am I being drawn to something deeper, perhaps gratitude or an action?

   ✤ In general, what is going on inside of me?

_____

_____

_____

PRAY

*JESUS, FIRE OF GOD'S LOVE, YOUR
HEART BURNS FOR EACH ONE OF US.
HELP ME REACH FOR THIS PURIFYING
FIRE SO THAT YOU MIGHT BURN AWAY
THE ENTANGLEMENTS THAT HAVE
GROWN AROUND MY OWN HEART.
HELP ME SEE MYSELF CLEARLY, THAT
I MIGHT ALSO SEE HOW YOU ARE
REACHING FOR ME. LIGHT ME ON
FIRE WITH YOUR LOVE, THAT I MIGHT
BURN FOR YOU ALONE. AMEN.*

FOURTH WEEK
OF LENT

A HEART RESCUED BY GOD

FOURTH WEEK OF LENT

SUNDAY

HE WHO IS THE "IMAGE OF THE INVISIBLE GOD" (COL 1:15) IS HIMSELF THE PERFECT MAN WHO HAS RESTORED IN THE CHILDREN OF ADAM THAT LIKENESS TO GOD WHICH HAD BEEN DISFIGURED EVER SINCE THE FIRST SIN. HUMAN NATURE, BY THE VERY FACT THAT IT WAS ASSUMED, NOT ABSORBED, IN HIM, HAS BEEN RAISED IN US ALSO TO A DIGNITY BEYOND COMPARE. FOR, BY HIS INCARNATION, HE, THE SON OF GOD, IN A CERTAIN WAY UNITED HIMSELF WITH EACH MAN. HE WORKED WITH HUMAN HANDS, HE THOUGHT WITH A HUMAN MIND. HE ACTED WITH A HUMAN WILL, AND WITH A HUMAN HEART HE LOVED.

GAUDIUM ET SPES, 22

PREPARE HIM ROOM

Last week, we celebrated the Feast of the Annunciation, which is the moment of the Incarnation, when Mary consented to God's plan so that the second person of the Trinity would be born in the world. I appreciate that oftentimes during Lent we are dragged back to Nazareth and the early life of Jesus through the celebration of the Annunciation. The image of Christ as an infant is important for us as we continue our journey with him into the wilderness of our own hearts.

Several years ago we were having a Christmas sing-along at our convent, and friends of mine who were fostering a baby girl came by for the festivities. They offered the baby girl to me to hold and gave me a bottle to feed her. As her foster mother handed her to me, she shared with me that the traumatic circumstances of her birth had impacted her early development, and for a while she did not have the natural reflex to suck like all infants do. This reflex is integral to a child surviving because it is the reflex that allows them to eat. I felt my heart break as I took her into my arms and watched her drink from the bottle. My heart broke in realizing that she was born with a broken heart, without a natural drive to thrive and live. It felt like a miracle to hold her and watch her do something she could not have done without healing.

This week we are going to reflect on God's longing and desire to heal our hearts and what that realistically looks like now and throughout our lives. I think, for now, it is good to realize that it is likely that the Redeemer of man, Christ, entered the world with a broken heart; his heart was broken for us, more aware of our need for him than we are. And as we pull him close, our own hearts ought to break, too, in the face of his vulnerability and willingness to be small. If he had been any greater, how would we be able to prepare him room?

REFLECT

1. Read the stories of the Annunciation (see Luke 1:26–38) and the Nativity (see Luke 2:1–7). Which person stands out to you?

2. Read the passages again, this time from the perspective of your chosen person. Now, use your imagination to reach out your senses. What do you see? Who and what is around you? What do you hear? Is it the sounds of people, birds, Jesus's voice, or even your own voice? What do you smell? Is there anything you taste?

3. Using your senses and placing yourself in the scene, read the passage a third time. What might God be telling you or showing you through this? Let this Scripture story open your heart to receive whatever message God might be revealing to you. Spend some time in silence, and listen to the Lord.

_____

_____

_____

_____

_____

_____

_____

_____

_____

_____

PRAY

GENTLE JESUS, YOU CAME INTO THIS WORLD AS AN INNOCENT, VULNERABLE INFANT TO SHOW US THE DEPTH OF YOUR LOVE. OPEN MY HEART TO MAKE ROOM FOR YOU AND TO RECEIVE YOUR HEALING. HELP ME TO BE VULNERABLE TO YOU AND TO REVEAL EVERY CREVICE OF MY HEART TO THE LIGHT OF YOUR LOVE. AMEN.

FOURTH WEEK OF LENT

MONDAY

THERE IS SOMETHING IN US THAT
DEMANDS THE REDEMPTIVE ACT, THAT
DEMANDS THAT WHAT FALLS AT LEAST BE
OFFERED THE CHANCE TO BE RESTORED.
THE READER OF TODAY LOOKS FOR THIS
MOTION, AND RIGHTLY SO, BUT WHAT HE
HAS FORGOTTEN IS THE COST OF IT. HIS
SENSE OF EVIL IS DILUTED OR LACKING
ALTOGETHER, AND SO HE HAS FORGOTTEN
THE PRICE OF RESTORATION. WHEN
HE READS A NOVEL, HE WANTS EITHER
HIS SENSE TORMENTED OR HIS SPIRITS
RAISED. HE WANTS TO BE TRANSPORTED,
INSTANTLY, EITHER TO MOCK DAMNATION
OR A MOCK INNOCENCE.

FLANNERY O'CONNOR, *MYSTERY AND
MANNERS: OCCASIONAL PROSE*

BANISH IDOLS

In some senses, we are still today at the bottom of Mount Sinai, growing impatient of waiting for God, and so we build an idol to worship. I have what will probably be an unpopular opinion, but here goes. I think the new golden calf is healing. I watch people spend large amounts of money on special healing retreats that last two to three days and go with expectations that this will be the silver bullet. I know instant miracles still happen, but what is also true is that even instant miracles need time to be lived into; there is a law of gradualism even in those cases. I find that in many cases we speak more of wounds and our healing work than we speak about Jesus and our relationship with him and his love for us. Healing has in a way become fashionable.

We at times have ventured into subtle Pelagianism, the heresy that asserts that God's grace is not entirely necessary for redemption. We do this by presuming that our experience of healing is a direct result of our own efforts, and if we are not where we want to be, then we simply have not done enough; we have not found the real wound. Some of us spend years navel gazing, looking for the special wound that will make it all make sense. All of this is an excursion from the way of the Cross.

There are only five glorified wounds in this world, and it is only by them and through them that we will be healed. There is no shortcut by way of Christ's wounds; there is no avoidance of the cost. Furthermore, healing is not the reason Christ is in relationship with us; the healing is an *effect* of the relationship, not the purpose. Christ's motivation for the relationship is only love, to be near us out of sheer goodness and love. The proximity has the effects of restoration.

I want to encourage you, as we reflect on Christ's healing presence in our hearts, to set aside a tendency to idolize your wounds and brokenness and the stories that explain them and instead idolize Christ himself. Dive deep into your *yes* to him, and he will do the rest. So when you finally do look at your wounds, the glory you see there will be his, which he has given you a share in—for by his wounds, yours are healed.

REFLECT

1. Reflect on your views of healing.
2. What would it be like for you to experience profound closeness to Christ, and yet at the same time not yet experience healing in areas where you wish to be healed?

_____

_____

_____

_____

_____

_____

_____

_____

_____

PRAY

*LORD, IT IS ONLY BY YOUR WOUNDS
THAT I AM HEALED. HELP ME TO SEE
YOUR GLORY IN MY WOUNDS AND TO
GROW EVER CLOSER TO YOU. MAY I
YEARN FOR INTIMACY WITH YOU FOR
ITS OWN SAKE—NOT MERELY SO THAT
I CAN BE HEALED, BUT SO THAT I CAN
BE SEEN BY YOU COMPLETELY AND
LOVE YOU MORE HEARTILY. AMEN.*

I KNOW THAT HE LOVES THE PRODIGAL SON, I HAVE HEARD HIS WORDS TO ST. MARY MAGDALEN, TO THE WOMAN TAKEN IN ADULTERY, AND TO THE WOMAN OF SAMARIA. NO ONE COULD FRIGHTEN ME, FOR I KNOW WHAT TO BELIEVE CONCERNING HIS MERCY AND HIS LOVE. AND I KNOW THAT ALL THAT MULTITUDE OF SINS WOULD DISAPPEAR IN AN INSTANT, EVEN AS A DROP OF WATER CAST INTO A FLAMING FURNACE.

ST. THÉRÈSE OF LISIEUX,
THE STORY OF A SOUL

TEND HIS GARDEN

My aunt who raised me is an avid gardener. What I know about avid gardeners is that they are always attentive to their gardens. My aunt would pause while walking to the car and tend to something in her garden briefly, would step outside while on the phone and pull a weed or admire a bloom, or give some extra care wherever she noted it was needed. I imagine this is sort of what it is like for Jesus as he heals and restores our hearts, as he roams about in this place he would like to call home.

Fr. Jacques Philippe wrote a small book on St. Thérèse of Lisieux titled *The Way of Trust and Love*, and in it he shared a remarkable truth learned from this Doctor of the Church. She believed that it was not our perfection or success that drew Jesus close to us or caused his gaze to rest upon us, to be attracted to us. Rather, our need for him is what draws him close and makes him attracted to us—much like how a gardener sets out into the garden that she loves. She of course admires what is going well in her garden, but above all she's there to lovingly tend. She hopes to notice what needs to be pruned, pulled up, watered, or where more light or shade could be helpful. The gardener brings order gently, joyfully, and sometimes slowly, over time.

All that you unpacked last week, the dark areas in your heart—Jesus wants to walk among all of it in the manner of an avid gardener. He is attracted to you in a similar way to one who lovingly and gratefully sets out to tend a garden.

Many times, I have sat before a tabernacle exasperated to still be broken in ways that I have begged God to heal me. One day, I finally perceived an insight in prayer from God; it was two simple statements: "You underestimate your need for me," and "What if I find joy in taking time with you?" In short, I underestimate the disarray of my soul! And yet, that very disarray is God's treasured garden to quietly and slowly tend.

REFLECT

1. Pray with Isaiah 58:11–12.
2. Reflect on whether you view healing and restoration as a joyful and loving encounter.
3. Is healing something you could waste time allowing God to do in you, or rather a task you are hoping God will hurry up and be done with already?

PRAY

*TENDER JESUS, YOU DESIRE TO
SPEND TIME IN THE WILD GARDEN OF
MY HEART, TO ADMIRE THE BLOOMS,
FERTILIZE THE SAPLINGS, AND PRUNE
THE WEEDS. HELP ME TO BE PATIENT
AS YOU CONDUCT YOUR WORK. MAY
I WELCOME YOUR PRESENCE AND
TRUST IN YOUR GENTLENESS. AMEN.*

FOURTH WEEK OF LENT

WEDNESDAY

LET US HOLD FAST THE
CONFESSION OF OUR HOPE
WITHOUT WAVERING, FOR HE
WHO PROMISED IS FAITHFUL.

HEBREWS 10:23

TAKE CAPTIVE YOUR THOUGHTS

Back to taking our thoughts captive. Last week, we spent some time just becoming aware of our thoughts and the patterns our negative thinking tends to fall into. I promised you that we would spend some time learning how to take those thoughts captive, and I want to make good on that promise. I shared previously about Marcus Warner's book *Understanding the Wounded Heart* and the WLVS model of understanding how the enemy takes command in areas of a wounded heart. Now, let's evict him, using more wisdom from Warner's work.

In his book, Warner teaches readers the CCC-C model as a way to take thoughts captive: confess, cancel, and command. He draws from the work of another minister and he adds one more: commit. We must begin by understanding that the enemy can only sow in our hearts what we give him permission to sow. We do not necessarily give the evil one permission on purpose, but we can do this inadvertently. Taking our thoughts captive revokes this permission and thus renounces the authority that was previously handed over. Here are the steps in a prayer of deliverance:

1. **Confess:** I confess that I have believed lies from the enemy, and I specifically renounce the lie that _____ _____.

2. **Cancel:** In the name of Jesus, I renounce that/those lie(s), and I ask Jesus to cancel the permission my belief in those lies has given to the enemy to have a place in my life.

3. **Command:** In the name of Jesus I command the evil spirits responsible for these lies and thoughts to leave now and take all their works and effects with them.

4. **Commit:** Lord, I commit myself to your truth and choose to believe what your Word says about me. I specifically

announce the truth that _____ *(include here the opposing truth of the lie previously renounced).*

And I pray all of this, in the name of the Father, and of the Son, and of the Holy Spirit. (See *Understanding the Wounded Heart,* 58–59.)

There was a particular thought pattern that had been bothering me for quite some time. I prayed this deliverance prayer, this prayer of taking thoughts captive as I wrote this for you, right before going to sleep (sometimes I forget to do the very things I am suggesting!). I woke up the next morning with marked peace and a certain quiet in the space of those thoughts. They were not completely gone, but something else was there. Perhaps it was the seeds of the Sower of Truth, who has faithfully stood by waiting for permission to fulfill his promise.

REFLECT

Return to the thought patterns and lies that surfaced in your prayer last week, and today take them captive by praying the CCC-C prayer of deliverance. Take it one lie at a time, specifically renouncing them one by one.

_____

_____

_____

_____

_____

_____

_____

_____

_____

_____

_____

_____

_____

_____

PRAY

_LORD, YOU ARE THE SOWER OF
TRUTH. HELP ME TO SEE THE LIES
I HAVE COME TO BELIEVE AND TO
RENOUNCE THEM COMPLETELY.
TEACH ME THE TRUTH YOU WILL FOR
ME AND GIVE ME THE GRACE TO
ANNOUNCE IT WHOLEHEARTEDLY.
AMEN._

THE LIGHT SHINES IN THE
DARKNESS, AND THE DARKNESS
HAS NOT OVERCOME IT.

JOHN 1:5

LIGHT UP THE DARKNESS

Shame is not guilt. Guilt is actually a healthy and appropriate response to having done something we know was wrong. Shame, however, sends the message that what I have done, or what has happened to me, has made me inherently wrong, unlovable, and not deserving of belonging and other good things. To put it in a Christian viewpoint, shame tells the lie that painful experiences or choices have disfigured the image and likeness of God in us. This is not possible; the image of God cannot be altered or disfigured in us, because it was given to us by the One who is unalterable; and the likeness, which was lost at original sin, was restored in the life, death, and Resurrection of Jesus.

Matt Maher's wife, Kristin Maher, published a children's book titled *The Awfulizer* about shame that frankly is useful for adults as well! I have two copies! In it she accomplishes a clinical feat that has baffled clinicians who serve children and teens for ages: how to help kids understand shame. Kristin's character, the Awfulizer, grows larger and more menacing the longer the boy in the book listens to the Awfulizer and keeps the voice of the Awfulizer a secret from those who can support and help him. The Awfulizer thrives in darkness, in silence, and in disconnection and isolation.

Once we say out loud the experiences we have had that have left us believing the lies that accompany shame, the dark cloud of shame can only scatter in the midst of this light. In EMDR therapy, we look back at former experiences and reprocess our view of them, unlearning lies connected to the experience and learning the truth about ourselves in light of those experiences. When I am providing EMDR therapy for a client, shame is often in the room; beliefs like "I do not deserve love," "I am powerless," "I cannot be trusted," and so much more surface while looking back at painful past events that are governing the present moment in a way they should not. I often tell clients that, when we look at the reason they are coming to counseling and then float back to the memories and experiences that inform their present experience, it is like we're turning on the lights in areas of their mind and heart where it has been dark for a while. It is startling at first, the brightness, but ultimately good.

REFLECT

1. Pray today with John 8:1–11.
2. Reflect not only on areas of your life where you experience shame, but also on times where you have perhaps shamed others, where you have stood in the place of their Awfulizer and fell into the temptation of defining them by their faults.

_____

_____

_____

_____

_____

_____

_____

_____

_____

_____

_____

_____

_____

_____

_____

_____

PRAY

*LORD OF LIGHT, YOU HAVE
CONQUERED DARKNESS SO WE MAY
LIVE IN YOUR LOVE. HELP ME TO
RECOGNIZE PLACES WHERE I HAVE
INTERNALIZED SHAME AND DOUBTED
MY WORTHINESS. WHERE PRIDE AND
A DESIRE FOR CONTROL STAND IN
MY WAY, GIVE ME HUMILITY AND
SURRENDER. FLOOD MY HEART WITH
THE LIGHT OF YOUR LOVE.*

FOURTH WEEK OF LENT

FRIDAY

I HAVE OVERCOME THE WORLD.

JOHN 16:33

MAKE PEACE WITH THE CROSS

I want to come back to the reality that many of us are living our lives with wounds and patterns of sin that we have begged God to heal, and we have not entirely received that healing.

I know firsthand what it is like to grow weary after having earnestly tried. Some of us pray every prayer, fast, go to Mass, Confession, and therapy. We do so much to show up and receive healing, and while the needle moves, it can all seem so slow. The reality that there are some wounds that will still be troubling us on our deathbed can be a source of sorrow and discouragement; we can find ourselves asking, "How long, O LORD?" (Ps 13:1).

Remember, he comes to rescue us so that we can be what he desires us to be. This requires that he live in us so that his presence can bring order to the wilderness. Perhaps these old tiresome wounds are, paradoxically, the very thing that has brought about the establishment of his reign in our hearts. Perhaps these happy faults allow us to make the bold statement that the kingdom of God is indeed in me! (See Luke 17:21.) Christ did not choose to build his kingdom in the recesses of your heart because of its perfection; he built it there because he had to in order that you might be one with him and go where he goes. He built it there so he wouldn't have to be without you, because he loves you, really loves you, and your present sufferings are not a sign that he has ceased to love you.

He has already won this fight. We are not waiting to see how this story is going to end. The baptismal waters never fail, the confessional is always a place of victory, the Holy Spirit is always poured out in the sacrament of Confirmation, and Jesus always shows up on the altar, Body, Blood, Soul, and Divinity at the words of consecration in the Mass . . . always. It is not *if* you will be healed—it is only *when*. So I would dare say, what you long for is already yours; ought we then worship him as if the healing we desire is a guarantee? He has overcome the world. This assurance gives us the opportunity to make peace with the cross as it shows up in our lives. This assurance makes not only his Cross lovely, but also ours.

REFLECT

1. Spend time today praying before a crucifix or before an image of the Holy Face of Jesus.
2. Where do you long for Jesus's healing? What would it mean for you to worship him as if the healing you desire is already yours?

_____

_____

_____

_____

_____

_____

_____

_____

_____

_____

_____

_____

_____

_____

_____

_____

_____

_____

PRAY

_KING OF MY HEART, YOU GAVE YOUR
BODY AND BLOOD IN ORDER TO
OVERCOME THE WILDERNESS AND
TO SAVE ME FROM BROKENNESS
HAVING THE FINAL SAY IN MY LIFE.
THANK YOU. HELP ME TO RECEIVE
THIS GIFT AND TO ACCEPT WHATEVER
SUFFERING YOU PERMIT ME TO
EXPERIENCE. AMEN._

FOURTH WEEK OF LENT

SATURDAY

ALMIGHTY AND EVER-LIVING GOD,
YOU SENT YOUR ONLY SON INTO THE
WORLD TO CAST OUT THE POWER OF
SATAN, SPIRIT OF EVIL, TO RESCUE MAN
FROM THE KINGDOM OF DARKNESS,
AND BRING HIM INTO THE SPLENDOR
OF YOUR KINGDOM OF LIGHT. WE PRAY
FOR THIS CHILD, SET HIM (HER) FREE
FROM ORIGINAL SIN, MAKE HIM (HER)
A TEMPLE OF YOUR GLORY, AND SEND
YOUR HOLY SPIRIT TO DWELL WITH HIM
(HER). WE ASK THIS THROUGH CHRIST
OUR LORD.

**FROM THE RITE OF BAPTISM
FOR ONE CHILD**

RENEW YOUR VOWS

If you were baptized in the Catholic Church as a child, this prayer was prayed over you. It is called the Prayer of Exorcism. In this prayer, the power of the Holy Spirit is invited in to shatter the chains of original sin and fill the child with light. This is who the baptized are: free children of God. The kingdom of darkness has no authority among the baptized that cannot be overcome with light. The baptized have been won for Christ and placed safely into his body.

We are going to break form a little bit this Saturday, and instead of reviewing the past week in the Reflect section of today, we're going to use today, if you are baptized, to renew our baptismal vows. It is this gift through which the door of your heart becomes accessible and Christ becomes your inheritance. It is through this gift that you can be assured that you will be healed. If you are not baptized, then simply pray this as a prayer, and as you pray, consider your call to the baptismal waters.

REFLECT

Renew now the vows of your own baptism. Reject sin; profess your faith in Christ Jesus. This is the faith of the Church. This is the faith in which you were baptized. After the renewal, use the lines provided to reflect on the experience.

Do you reject Satan? _____
(write in the words "I do" in each blank)

And all his works? _____

And all his empty promises? _____

Do you believe in God, the Father almighty, creator of heaven and earth? _____

Do you believe in Jesus Christ, his only Son, our Lord, who was born of the Virgin Mary, was crucified, died, and was buried, rose from the dead, and is now seated at the right hand of the Father? _____

Do you believe in the Holy Spirit, the holy catholic Church, the communion of saints, the forgiveness of sins, the resurrection of the body, and the life everlasting? _____

This is our faith. This is the faith of the Church. We are proud to profess it, in Christ Jesus our Lord. Amen. (The Rite of Baptism for One Child.)

PRAY

*COME, HOLY SPIRIT, OVERCOME
MY HEART WITH YOUR LIGHT. HELP
ME TO LIVE IN FREEDOM AND TO
RECEIVE MY INHERITANCE AS A CHILD
OF GOD. I LOVE YOU, LORD. AMEN.*

FIFTH WEEK
OF LENT

A HEART
POURED OUT
WITH GOD

FIFTH WEEK OF LENT

SUNDAY

MAN CANNOT LIVE WITHOUT
LOVE. HE REMAINS A BEING
THAT IS INCOMPREHENSIBLE
FOR HIMSELF, HIS LIFE IS
SENSELESS, IF LOVE IS NOT
REVEALED TO HIM, IF HE DOES
NOT ENCOUNTER LOVE, IF HE
DOES NOT EXPERIENCE IT AND
MAKE IT HIS OWN, IF HE DOES
NOT PARTICIPATE INTIMATELY
IN IT.

ST. JOHN PAUL II, *REDEMPTOR HOMINIS*

LEAVE THE WILDERNESS

This week we are going to turn our attention to the other part of the relational dynamic that allows a person to become what and who God desires him to be. Sometimes, when we hear phrases like "Man cannot live without love" or "Man cannot find himself except through a sincere gift of himself," our attention can go to reflecting on how we are being loved and how we are being received as gift. This is a good response, and we absolutely need to reflect on those things; and it is more of both/and than either/or. We must also reflect on how we are giving love and how we are receiving others as gift. How are we helping others to comprehend their great dignity and worth? For it is not being loved alone that makes us understand exactly who we are and what we were made for; this is fully known in giving love, in self-donation. Otherwise, our pursuit of healing would be a scandal and make a mockery of the Cross, for "You are not your own" (1 Cor 6:19). The healing and graces we receive are also not our own; they are for the building of the kingdom. Also, complete healing can only be achieved when we give what we have received.

Christ's restoration of the wilderness within our hearts is an ongoing restoration of the likeness of God we were given, of our ability to be like God. This means when all is said and done, our hearts will beat like and with his and will be poured out like his. For, as St. Athanasius wrote, "God became man so that man might become God."

It would be nice, and overall exceptionally consoling, to stop at the level of abiding with God in our hearts—to spend all our time in prayer learning to love him for his faithfulness in the wilderness, fixed constantly on what he needs to tend now, on inviting him into to ever deeper recesses of our hearts. But this sole preoccupation would be futile and a miscarriage of the Gospel. We will not be judged on how well we invited Jesus into our hearts; we will be judged on how we stewarded his miraculous work in the wilderness within. As St. John of the Cross said, "In the evening of life, we will be judged on love alone." Let us prepare this week, hand-in-hand with Jesus, to come out of the wilderness, to live the Gospel, and ultimately to walk faithfully with him on the road to Calvary.

REFLECT

1. Pray with the Gospel of Matthew, chapter 25.
2. The corporal works of mercy are to feed the hungry, give drink to the thirsty, shelter the homeless, clothe the naked, visit the sick, visit the imprisoned, and bury the dead. The spiritual works of mercy are to instruct the ignorant, counsel the doubtful, admonish sinners, forgive offenses, comfort the afflicted, bear wrongs patiently, and pray for the living and the dead. Reflect today on one or two of these works that you feel called to grow in living out.

PRAY

*GOD OUR FATHER, YOU SENT
YOUR SON INTO THE WILDERNESS
OF OUR HUMANITY AS A SIGN OF
YOUR LOVE AND TO GIVE US A WAY
TO PARTICIPATE IN YOUR LOVE.
AS I DEEPEN MY EXPERIENCE OF
YOUR LOVE THIS LENT, GIVE ME A
SACRIFICIAL HEART SO THAT I CAN
SHARE THIS LOVE WITH OTHERS
GENEROUSLY. AMEN.*

FIFTH WEEK OF LENT

MONDAY

EVERY MAN AND WOMAN IS A
MISSION. THAT IS THE REASON
FOR OUR LIFE ON THIS EARTH.

**POPE FRANCIS, WORLD MISSION DAY
MESSAGE, 2018**

YOU ARE A MISSION

Similar to the fact that we *are* a relationship, we do not have a mission, but we *are* a mission. The word *mission* means "to be sent, or sending." So, our very identity is "one who is sent." To where?

One morning, not long after my first vows, I sat down to plan my day. My ministry included marketing our retreat center in the dioceses closest to our convent. I was planning to visit several parishes to drop off some literature, and I decided to make my Holy Hour in a new perpetual Adoration chapel at one of the parishes I was visiting. The Adoration chapel was not finished, so I prayed in the church. The day was going perfectly as planned. I sat down right on time for my Holy Hour, and within minutes a woman walked in and dropped to the floor right at the steps of the sanctuary. I looked around for someone there who could maybe help her and realized that person was me! I walked to her, and as I drew closer I heard her praying in Spanish, a language I speak sparsely. I was able to ask her if there was something she needed, and she looked at me and said, in Spanish, "My mother is dead." I sat down on the floor with her and held her hand as she cried, and we prayed. After a few minutes I felt a tap on my shoulder, and a Vietnamese woman said to me, "Sister, when you finish praying with her, will you come pray with me? My brother died, and he did not go to church." The woman I was with on the floor gave me a sign that it was alright to go, and the other woman took my hand and led me outside to the columbarium. She placed my hand on a plot with her brother's name etched on it and said, "Sister, please pray." And so, I prayed for her brother.

Where are we sent? Wherever God desires, at any given moment on any given day. As a religious Sister, this radical presence is more pronounced than it is for others. This is the purpose of a habit, so even strangers know they have a right to a more radical availability from me. But we are all called to surrender to the mystery of being sent, not according to our own plans, but according to God's desires.

REFLECT

1. Pray with John 17:18–21.
2. What thoughts and feelings do you have when you think of being sent in a manner that may not be according to your plans?
3. What memories come to mind of experiences of being sent?

_____

_____

_____

_____

_____

_____

_____

_____

_____

_____

PRAY

*FATHER OF MERCY, YOU SENT YOUR
SON AMONG US TO PROCLAIM
LIBERTY TO CAPTIVES AND TO
RESTORE SIGHT TO THE BLIND.
OUR BAPTISM JOINS US TO JESUS'S
MISSION. HELP ME TO BE AVAILABLE
TO THOSE WHO NEED YOUR MERCY
AND TO BE A CONDUIT FOR YOUR
COMPASSION AND JUSTICE. AMEN.*

FIFTH WEEK OF LENT

TUESDAY

I AM THE VINE, YOU ARE THE
BRANCHES. HE WHO ABIDES
IN ME, AND I IN HIM, HE IT
IS THAT BEARS MUCH FRUIT,
FOR APART FROM ME YOU CAN
DO NOTHING.

JOHN 15:5

HE IS THE VINE

The foundress of my religious community is blessed in the Church. Bl. Mary of Jesus the Good Shepherd is her religious name, and Frances Siedliska is her baptismal name. We have her relics in almost all of our convents, and there is one style of reliquary that we use that is my favorite. The entire reliquary is golden colored, and it looks like a tree on a stand, with branches twisting and growing upward. In the middle of the tree and vines at the top of the reliquary is the world. Wrapping upward around the trunk of the tree, moving toward the world, is a banner that reads, *"Mundum universum in est diffusus amor dei infinitus Nazareth"* (The infinite love of God came out of Nazareth and spread to the whole world). The base of the reliquary from which the love of Nazareth grows out and upward from is your heart. Love still comes out and grows out of Nazareth today and spreads through the whole world, through you, as long as you abide in Jesus.

There is no such thing as being poured out for mission apart from Christ and a life of prayer. A deep interior life must be the source of mission, or what we are sharing and pouring on the world is our own ego and vainglory, and we are doomed to wither and die. The perfect champion of social justice is the one who prays daily and abides with Jesus in the scriptures and the sacraments. The perfect champion of prayer is the one who rises from their prayer corners and chapels and allows the treasures God has worked in their heart to bear fruit and be poured out, even to the ends of the earth (see Acts 1:8). It is important to me that, as we reflect on what God is doing and has been doing to be poured out from our hearts, we do not fall into the trap of allowing mission to dismiss prayer. We cannot have one without the other. Our hearts are not poured out *for* God; they are poured out *with* God, in him, through him, and with him, for the sake of his kingdom and for others. Apart from him, we can do nothing.

REFLECT

1. Pray with John 15:1–17.
2. When it is not Lent, how is your prayer life?
3. What plans can you make beyond Lent to pray daily or deepen your daily prayer and efforts to abide in Jesus?

_____

_____

_____

_____

_____

_____

_____

_____

_____

_____

_____

_____

PRAY

*JESUS, YOU ARE THE VINE WHO
BRINGS US LIFE. HELP ME GROW
DEEP ROOTS IN YOUR PRESENCE SO
THAT MY LIFE MIGHT BEAR FRUIT
FOR OTHERS. AS I LEARN TO ABIDE
IN YOUR LOVE THIS LENT, HELP ME
SUSTAIN MY PRACTICE OF PRAYER
AND MY MISSION OF SERVICE
THROUGH THIS SEASON TO THE REST
OF THE YEAR. AMEN.*

FIFTH WEEK OF LENT

WEDNESDAY

POPE ST. LEO THE GREAT SAYS THAT
"THE TERM 'NEIGHBOR' INCLUDES NOT
ONLY THOSE WITH WHOM WE HAVE TIES
OF FRIENDSHIP OR FAMILY, BUT ALL OUR
FELLOW MEN WITH WHOM WE SHARE A
COMMON NATURE." . . . OUR LOVE IS NOT
TO BE CONFUSED WITH SENTIMENTALITY
OR MERE GOOD FELLOWSHIP, NOR WITH
THAT SOMEWHAT QUESTIONABLE ZEAL TO
HELP OTHERS IN ORDER TO CONVINCE
OURSELVES OF OUR SUPERIORITY.
RATHER, IT MEANS LIVING IN PEACE WITH
OUR NEIGHBOR, VENERATING THE IMAGE
OF GOD THAT IS FOUND IN EACH AND
EVERY MAN.

ST. JOSEMARÍA ESCRIVÁ,
FRIENDS OF GOD, 230

LOVE YOUR NEIGHBOR

Between podcasts, YouTube, social media, and personality-driven apostolates, we are now able to carefully curate our experience of the Gospel; who we follow and listen to determines how and when we are challenged. This careful curation allows us to be almost certain to avoid being challenged in ways we do not prefer. If for some reason God is able to break through our carefully curated experience of "Church," we then tend to either recoil and flee or attack and cancel; we revolt against what might break down the walls of the false church we have built. When the water flowed from the threshold of the Temple (see Ezekiel 47:1) and when the font poured forth from Jesus's heart (see John 19:34), this stream of mercy did not skirt around anyone it approached who wasn't related to Jesus or didn't look like Jesus, act like him, or share his preferences. The font of mercy approaches all; and if we are privileged for it to now flow from our own heart, then we must approach all too. I am not saying we all need to be best friends or need to place ourselves in harm's way. I am speaking of having a kinship with our neighbors and recognizing God in them.

In *Friends of God*, St. Josemaría Escrivá goes on to say, "If we must also love our enemies . . . we have all the more reason for loving those who are simply distant from us, those whom we find less attractive, those who seem the opposite of you or me on account of their language, culture or upbringing."

I live in a small town that has its fair share of Catholic cliques. In fact, I am a member of a couple of the cliques, and am super comfortable there. I am also a spouse of Jesus Christ and a counselor. There have definitely been people walking through the doors of my counseling office who did not belong to my clique, who perhaps belonged to my least favorite clique. I have been personally grateful for this challenge, which is saving me from inadvertently shutting God out of my heart because I prefer a God and a religion that does not prune, does not pinch, does not refine. St. Teresa of Calcutta once said, "Love to be real, it must cost—it must hurt—it must empty us of self." The group you are most resistant to may, in fact, be where you are called to serve.

REFLECT

1. Pray with Luke 10:25–37.
2. What does love of neighbor look like for you now, and how might you be called to grow, particularly in service to those with whom you do not feel in agreement?

PRAY

*GOD OUR FATHER, YOU GATHER YOUR
PEOPLE INTO ONE FAMILY. HELP ME
TO SEE OTHERS AS MY BROTHERS
AND SISTERS IN YOU, ESPECIALLY
THOSE WHO SEEM MOST DIFFERENT
FROM ME. GRANT ME COURAGE TO
BRIDGE DISTANCE WHEN I SEE IT AND
TO WELCOME THE CHALLENGE OF
LOVING UNCONDITIONALLY AS YOU
DO. AMEN.*

FIFTH WEEK OF LENT

THURSDAY

SO THAT SHE CAN FULFILL HER MISSION,
THE HOLY SPIRIT "BESTOWS UPON [THE
CHURCH] VARIED HIERARCHIC AND
CHARISMATIC GIFTS, AND IN THIS WAY
DIRECTS HER." HENCEFORWARD THE
CHURCH, ENDOWED WITH THE GIFTS
OF HER FOUNDER AND FAITHFULLY
OBSERVING HIS PRECEPTS OF CHARITY,
HUMILITY AND SELF-DENIAL, RECEIVES
THE MISSION OF PROCLAIMING
AND ESTABLISHING AMONG ALL
PEOPLES THE KINGDOM OF CHRIST
AND OF GOD, AND SHE IS ON EARTH
THE SEED AND THE BEGINNING OF
THAT KINGDOM.

CATECHISM OF THE CATHOLIC CHURCH,
768, QUOTING *LUMEN GENTIUM*, 4

BE A GOOD STEWARD

If you are a gift, then you are called to be a good steward of yourself! Self-stewardship can be understood from multiple angles. One would be knowing what your gifts are and how you are called to share them with your family, friends, and community. Another angle includes understanding how boundaries are an expression of love and service.

In the Church, we speak of gifts within a person as their charisms. Charisms are an extraordinary power given to a Christian by the Holy Spirit for the good of the Church. We possess distinct and unique powers given to us by the third person of the Blessed Trinity, and it is important that we know them, can name them, and strive to increase our intentionality regarding placing them at the service of the Church.

An image comes to mind. I am fascinated by the fact that one plant can thrive in one place and suffer in another. When I moved to east Texas from the Dallas area, it was striking to me how much more vibrant and plush the flowers and plants were in east Texas, just two hours from Dallas. I inquired about the cause and was told that the soil of the east Texas ground is unique and makes for a very life-giving home for beautiful plants and trees, specifically hydrangea, roses, and azaleas.

God makes us with very specific soil that has the ability to appropriate specific charisms from the Holy Spirit. We are unique and unrepeatable, necessary members of the Body of Christ. No one can contribute to the building of the kingdom what we can, and so we have a great responsibility, because our purpose unfulfilled will be missed in the Body of Christ.

Living out our charisms must be done with a clear understanding of our boundaries. The four types of boundaries are mental, emotional, physical, and internal. The common barrier to setting boundaries is fear—fear of being judged, of conflict, of hurting feelings, and of losing a relationship. I believe boundaries are a form of communicating to others our own dignity *and* theirs. They are a pastoral and loving tool that concretizes the theological truth of our uniqueness and unrepeatability. Struggling to keep and have them places at risk stewardship of not only our own gifts, but also those of another.

REFLECT

1. Pray with Psalm 139 today.
2. If you have never completed a charisms inventory, complete the charisms inventory available at https://www.new-manonline.org/theologyontap-gifts-test or any free online assessment in order to identify your charisms. You may be surprised by your results! Is there an underused charism that you have?
3. How have healthy boundaries (or a lack of them) helped (or harmed) your ability to use your gifts for the good of the Church?
4. Visit the *Wilderness Within* webpage to review a handout on boundaries: www.avemariapress.com/private/page/wilderness-within-resources.

_____

_____

_____

_____

_____

_____

_____

PRAY

_ALMIGHTY CREATOR, YOU CREATED
EACH OF US WITH GREAT CARE,
AND YOU CONTINUE TO CALL US
TO PARTICIPATE IN THE COMING OF
YOUR KINGDOM. HELP ME GROW IN
SELF-AWARENESS AND CONFIDENCE
IN THE GIFTS YOUR HOLY SPIRIT
HAS GRANTED ME, AND GRANT ME
WISDOM TO SEE THE SPECIFIC WORK
YOU ARE CALLING ME TO. KEEP
ME CENTERED IN YOUR LOVE AND
TRUTH. AMEN._

FIFTH WEEK OF LENT

FRIDAY

THOSE WHO PROMOTE THIS
DEVOTION [TO THE SACRED
HEART] WILL HAVE THEIR NAMES
WRITTEN IN MY HEART, NEVER
TO BE EFFACED.

**JESUS TO ST. MARGARET MARY
ALACOQUE**

BECOME A FONT OF MERCY

Servant of God Julia Greeley is someone whom I came to know about shortly before my final vows. She was enslaved in Missouri, and upon being freed she went to live in Denver, Colorado. There she became known as the Angel of Charity. I was tasked with writing an essay about her for a book on the six Black Catholic Americans on the road to sainthood, and after reflecting on her life, I chose to call her an usher of the font of mercy. Julia Greeley was a daily communicant with a deep devotion to the Sacred Heart, the Blessed Sacrament, and the Blessed Virgin. Although she did not have much, Julia would go out at night with food and other goods in a red wagon and give them to others who had unmet needs. She also ministered to firefighters, sharing with them about devotion to the Sacred Heart and inviting them into her ministry of serving the poor. She was devoted, she was simple, she humbly served, and she had a desire to console the Heart of Jesus. I know now that I called her by the wrong title on that first opportunity to write about her. She is not an usher—she is a conduit.

Ezekiel chapter 47 includes the beautiful image of water flowing from the right side (south side) of the Temple. John 19:34 reads, "One of the soldiers pierced his side with a spear, and at once there came out blood and water." Jesus's pierced side is his right side. The piercing reached his heart, opening up a glorified wound from which blood and water now. As promised in Ezekiel, this blood and water gives life to all, our font of mercy.

This font is unleashed in us through the sacraments and through allowing God to take over in the wilderness of our hearts and order them and arrange them in a manner like his own. Julia did not usher the flow of this merciful font; it passed right through her. At night, as she pulled her wagon in service of the poor. Each morning she walked to daily Mass, fasting and saying when others offered her food, "My Communion is my breakfast." When she was bold enough to minister to local firefighters, the font of mercy passed right through her. Her name is written in the heart of Christ, because she allowed him to fill her heart with his love, so that it might flow out to those she encountered.

REFLECT

1. Pray with Ezekiel 47:1–12.
2. Where are you being called to be poured out (or to show mercy) and you may have been hesitant to do so?
3. Pray through the intercession of Servant of God Julia Greeley to deepen your freedom to have the font of mercy unleashed in you.

PRAY

*JESUS, FONT OF THE FATHER'S
MERCY, YOU ARE A LIFE-GIVING
STREAM POURED OUT FOR THE
WORLD. YOU IMMERSED EACH OF
US IN THIS FLOWING LOVE AT OUR
BAPTISM. NOW POUR YOUR GRACE
INTO OUR LIVES, THAT WE MIGHT
BE A CONDUIT OF YOUR PRESENCE
TO THOSE WHO ARE THIRSTY AND
OVERBURDENED. OPEN ME THAT I
MIGHT BECOME A FONT OF LOVE
TOO. AMEN.*

FIFTH WEEK OF LENT

SATURDAY

THE MISSION OF THE CHRISTIAN IN THE WORLD IS A MISSION FOR ALL, A MISSION OF SERVICE, WHICH EXCLUDES NO-ONE; IT REQUIRES GREAT GENEROSITY AND IN PARTICULAR THE GAZE AND HEART TURNED HEAVENWARD TO INVOKE THE LORD'S HELP. THERE IS SO MUCH NEED FOR CHRISTIANS WHO BEAR WITNESS TO THE GOSPEL WITH JOY IN EVERYDAY LIFE. THE DISCIPLES, SENT BY JESUS, "RETURNED WITH JOY." WHEN WE DO THIS, OUR HEART FILLS WITH JOY.

POPE FRANCIS, ANGELUS, JULY 3, 2016, QUOTING LUKE 10:17

STATE YOUR MISSION

I saw on a message board someone once ask the question, "What is the mission statement of the Catholic Church?" Another person responded with paragraph 849 of the *Catechism*:

> *The missionary mandate.* "Having been divinely sent to the nations that she might be 'the universal sacrament of salvation,' the Church, in obedience to the command of her founder and because it is demanded by her own essential universality, strives to preach the Gospel to all men": "Go therefore and make disciples of all nations, baptizing them in the name of the Father and of the Son and of the Holy Spirit, teaching them to observe all that I have commanded you; and Lo, I am with you always, until the close of the age."

It doesn't get clearer than that. But as we reflected a few days ago, the Holy Spirit fills the world with various gifts and charisms to help us as a Church move toward the building of God's kingdom.

One day at our retreat center in Texas, we had a family retreat. About one hundred people from several families attended, and we worked with them together, and then also split them into groups based on ages and did some age- and role-specific work. No Sister was left out; everyone had to bring their gifts to the table in order to work with all the families there. Sr. Mary Louise, who was our spiritual leader in the whole effort, had as the end goal that each family write a mission statement at the end of the retreat, seeking to answer the questions, What is your mission as a family? For what purpose did God call you as a family by name? It was beautiful to see what each family came up with and how their charisms intermingled into a common purpose. Each charism was an expression of the overall mandate to go and make disciples as well as a reminder to each family that they are not their own but a gift to the Church and for the Church.

REFLECT

1. Make a list of your unique charisms, and describe your prayer life from which your call to be poured out in self-donation flows.
2. Name areas you may be called to allow yourself to be poured out and are resisting.
3. Now, what is your unique mission in the Church, in your own words?

_____

_____

_____

_____

_____

_____

_____

_____

_____

_____

_____

PRAY

SPIRIT OF LIFE, YOU CALL US TO PROCLAIM THE GOOD NEWS OF GOD'S LOVE BY OUR WORDS AND DEEDS. EMPOWER ME WITH COURAGE AND JOY, THAT I MIGHT BRING THIS LOVE TO THE PEOPLE WHOM YOU PLACE IN MY LIFE, ESPECIALLY THOSE IN MY EVERYDAY CIRCUMSTANCES. DEEPEN MY GENEROSITY, AND HELP ME TO TRUST THAT YOU WILL BE WITH ME WHENEVER I STEP OUTSIDE OF MYSELF IN LOVE. AMEN.

HOLY WEEK

A HEART UNITED WITH CHRIST

HOLY WEEK

PALM SUNDAY

LET MY EYES RUN DOWN WITH
TEARS NIGHT AND DAY, AND
LET THEM NOT CEASE, FOR
THE VIRGIN DAUGHTER OF MY
PEOPLE IS STRUCK DOWN WITH
A CRUSHING BLOW, WITH A VERY
GRIEVOUS WOUND.

JEREMIAH 14:17

ASCEND TO JERUSALEM

We have arrived at the holiest week of the year. It is a week fashioned for well-formed hearts, and you have spent Lent striving to make yours just that, a well-formed heart. It is holy, because it is our opportunity to live a profound devotion to the Passion of Jesus Christ and his Resurrection. However, the main feature that causes this week to be holy is not the Cross in and of itself, nor is it the Resurrection. The defining feature that makes this week holy is love. In *Jesus of Nazareth*, when reflecting on Jesus's entrance into Jerusalem on Palm Sunday, Pope Benedict XVI notes that Jesus's entire pilgrim journey is an ascent from the Sea of Galilee, 690 feet below sea level, to Jerusalem, 2,500 feet above sea level. Pope Benedict XVI writes that Jesus's steps "point to an inner ascent that is accomplished in the outward climb." Jesus's ascent is the ascent that the Letter to the Hebrews describes as going up, not to a sanctuary made by human hands, but to heaven itself. This ascent into God's presence leads via the Cross—it is the ascent toward "loving . . . to the end" (Jn 13:1), which is the real mountain of God.

I want to thank you for taking this Lenten journey with me. It was not typical in many ways, but we have been faithful to the very first mandate of this season: rend your hearts. You have done this. You have canvassed the fabric and foundation of your heart, love. You have delved into its purpose: relationship, most profoundly lived out in mission. You have faced the brokenness that each of our hearts is marked by and have grown in your capacity to be healed in the broken and wounded places in the wilderness of the heart.

Throughout Lent, we have obediently allowed God to love us, inviting him into our hearts. Now, let us return that love by ascending with him to love to the end. Today, we follow him into Jerusalem. Reading one verse past the gospel proclaimed at the procession of palms, you will see that Jesus weeps at the sight of Jerusalem, similar to how God wept in the book of the prophet Jeremiah. This week, let's strive to move beyond spending Holy Week feeling sad for Jesus, even beyond simply feeling grateful for Jesus. This week, let us feel and experience it all *with* Jesus.

REFLECT

1. Pray with the Gospel of Luke 19:28–41. Imagine yourself entering Jerusalem with Jesus and seeing his weeping at the sight of the city. In your prayer, try to think what Jesus must have thought and felt that caused his tears.
2. If Jesus entered your city today, what would cause him to weep?

_____

_____

_____

_____

_____

_____

_____

_____

_____

PRAY

*GOD OF LOVE, YOU SENT YOUR SON
INTO THE WORLD SO THAT WE COULD
BE PARTAKERS IN YOUR DIVINE LIFE.
HELP ME TO ENTER FULLY INTO
THIS MYSTERY DURING HOLY WEEK
AND TO ACCEPT ALL THAT YOU WISH
TO TEACH ME. INSPIRE ME TO LIFT
UP MY HEART AND TO LOVE YOU
COMPLETELY. AMEN.*

HOLY WEEK

MONDAY

THE ONE WHO "WENT ABOUT DOING
GOOD AND HEALING" NOW HIMSELF
SEEMS TO MERIT THE GREATEST MERCY
AND TO APPEAL FOR MERCY, WHEN HE
IS ARRESTED, ABUSED, CONDEMNED,
SCOURGED, CROWNED WITH THORNS,
WHEN HE IS NAILED TO THE CROSS AND
DIES AMIDST AGONIZING TORMENTS.
IT IS THEN THAT HE PARTICULARLY
DESERVES MERCY FROM THE PEOPLE
TO WHOM HE HAS DONE GOOD, AND
HE DOES NOT RECEIVE IT.

ST. JOHN PAUL II, *RICH IN MERCY*

BE DEVOTED

In today's gospel reading, Mary, the sister of Lazarus and Martha, is back at Jesus's feet, this time anointing his feet with a pound of costly perfume made of pure nard that she bought with her own money in preparation for Jesus's burial. She anoints his feet and dries them with her own hair, despite the complaints of Judas, who puts her act of love and devotion toward Jesus at odds with service to the poor. It is not.

Last week we reflected on the importance of mission, self-donation, and service. These are essential to the Christian life. Yet, these behaviors are absolutely worthless apart from love of Jesus. I often encounter Catholics who struggle to be in balance. Either there is a heavy focus on devotion, liturgy, and worship while a sense of service remains lacking; or there is a heavy focus on activism, justice, and works of mercy while lacking a sense of real longing to simply be at the feet of Jesus, loving him through prayer and worship. Mary, the sister of Lazarus and Martha, is the model disciple: at the feet of Jesus, with her eyes on Jesus, offering him her devotion by pouring out costly oil. This positions her to continue to encounter her Lord as he appears in those she seeks to serve in his name.

In service to the poor, what we aim to do is continue to kneel before the feet of Jesus, because in them we encounter him. I believe Jesus looked upon his friend at dinner that evening and was grateful that she saw him, that she was attentive to his needs, that she was aware of his need for preparation for burial, that she was willing to bestow costly devotion upon him. She showed God mercy.

All service is best born in devotion to and love for Jesus; then it consoles his heart and quenches his thirst. Continue to walk closely to Jesus, seeking to know his heart and mind in these final days of his life and seeking to be a source of consolation for him. Notice that where Mary is, at the feet of whom she loves, Jesus will be in the same place, just a few days later.

REFLECT

1. Pray with John 12:1–11. Imagine yourself there in the home at Bethany as the scene unfolds. In your prayer, put yourself in the position of Jesus. Imagine what he must have thought and felt while his feet were being anointed.
2. Is there a costly devotion that you are being called to offer to Jesus as you continue to make the inner ascent to the Cross? Consider clearing some things off your calendar to quiet your week, and limit or eliminate your time spent consuming media if you have not already.
3. Reflect on how you can show Jesus mercy.

_____

_____

_____

_____

_____

_____

_____

_____

PRAY

LORD OF ENDLESS MERCY, DEEPEN MY DEVOTION TO YOU, AND SHOW ME HOW YOU'RE CALLING ME TO SERVE YOU. TEACH ME TO CONSOLE YOUR HEART AND QUENCH YOUR THIRST SO THAT I CAN BRING YOUR MERCY INTO THIS WORLD IN A TANGIBLE WAY. GUIDE MY HEART AND MY ACTIONS SO THAT I MAY BE YOUR HANDS AND FEET. AMEN.

HOLY WEEK

TUESDAY

AND WE ALL, WITH UNVEILED
FACES, BEHOLDING THE GLORY
OF THE LORD, ARE BEING
CHANGED INTO HIS LIKENESS
FROM ONE DEGREE OF GLORY
TO ANOTHER; FOR THIS COMES
FROM THE LORD WHO IS
THE SPIRIT.

2 CORINTHIANS 3:18

FILL THE EMPTY SPACE

In today's gospel reading, Jesus reclines at table with his friends. Judas, one his closest followers, is identified as the one who will betray Jesus. Jesus explains to his disciples remaining at the table with him after Judas departs that he is going to a place where they cannot follow, for the first time since they began to follow him. Simon Peter makes a promise not to betray Jesus and to give his life for him; this is a promise Jesus knows Simon Peter will not keep.

Jesus has a perfectly rended heart. When we were asked to rend our hearts at the outset of Lent, it was ultimately an invitation to allow our hearts to be formed into Christ's own heart. Rended hearts are actually more susceptible to wounds. I think this is the reason we grow hardened hearts and lock up the doors to our wilderness within. It hurts to feel alone and to be betrayed. Healing does not reduce the likeliness of feeling these pains; healing causes us to feel them more sincerely. But healing also gives us an opportunity to abide in God's love in a manner likened to Jesus's own experience, which gives all suffering meaning and a destination. Abiding in the Father's love transforms the final destination of all pain into love.

In the previous weeks I failed to talk about attachment styles, or the ways we learn to love. We learn attachment styles from our parents, and since there are no perfect parents, there are rarely children who have perfectly secure attachment styles! We often think it is the things that happened to us that shape attachment style (avoidant, anxious-preoccupied, or fearful-anxious); this is partially true. Yet, it is also the things that *didn't* happen that shape our attachment styles—the times we did not receive support or comfort. Jesus brought the love of the Father into your heart this Lent to bring healing regarding not only what happened but also what didn't happen. In a sense, he comes to your heart so that what did not happen can now happen; he fills this empty space with love. Now, enter into his rended heart. Sit with Jesus, deepening your understanding of him in this sacred week. The people who are most important to him are growing further away from him. He takes all that on, it hurts him deeply, and yet, he continues his ascent—he does not close off his heart.

REFLECT

1. Pray with the Gospel of John 13:21–33, 36–38. Imagine yourself there at the table as the scene unfolds. Perhaps imagine yourself as one of the disciples named in the scripture story.
2. In your prayer try to think what Jesus must have thought and felt during this exchange.
3. What small and simple offering can you make today as a sign to Jesus that you see him and desire to remain faithful to him?

PRAY

*GOD OF LOVE, YOU NEVER CEASE
TRANSFORMING ALL PAIN INTO LOVE.
TEACH ME TO ABIDE IN YOU ALWAYS
AND TO TRUST IN YOUR LOVING
CARE. SHOW ME HOW YOU WANT TO
LOVE ME, AND HELP ME TO REMAIN
FAITHFUL TO YOU IN ALL THAT I DO.
AMEN.*

WEDNESDAY

WE ARE NOT DISGRACED BY OUR
SUFFERINGS, WE ARE GRACED.

PETER KREEFT, *FOOD FOR THE SOUL*

LOVE HIM WELL

During Holy Week, beginning on Palm Sunday and extending through today, the first daily Mass readings are taken from the book of the prophet Isaiah. These passages are described as being depictions of Jesus as the Suffering Servant or the Suffering Servant Songs. Today's passage recounts the physical humiliation that the Suffering Servant endures: "I gave my back to those who struck me, and my cheeks to those who pulled out the beard; I hid not my face from shame and spitting" (Is 50:6). These words are reminiscent of what is to come on Good Friday as Jesus endures his Passion.

I read a unique poem once, written by a Jesuit priest, about the Good Friday mocking of Jesus. The poem was titled "Moron," by Peter Steele, SJ, and it is written from the perspective of the soldiers who were mocking and beating Jesus. In the poem the landing of the reeds that beat Jesus on his flesh are described as an achievement; they indeed are, but not in the way the soldiers imagined. When I prayed with this poem, what I realized was that as each blow landed, because of who received the blow and the manner in which he received it, each blow became an additional step on the ascent to the mountaintop of God, salvific love. Indeed, what an achievement. Peter Kreeft, when reflecting on this same passage, draws attention to the use of the word *therefore*: "The Lord God helps me; therefore I have not been confounded" (Is 50:7). Kreeft writes, "Notice the therefore, being on the Lord's side changes everything; whoever is doing his will is never disgraced but always graced. Sometimes the grace comes in the form of joy, and sometimes it comes in the form of suffering. Suffering is not a disgrace. Martyrdom is not a disgrace" (*Food for the Soul: Reflections on the Mass Readings*, 222).

In today's first reading we see the Suffering Servant set his face like "flint" (Is 50:7), which means with persevering determination. We see similar words used later in the Gospel of Luke, chapter 9, when Jesus plans to head to Jerusalem; his face is described as *set* toward Jerusalem, the high point of his ascent. His suffering is an achievement, for you and for all. Because you have not spent these days submerged in your own perfectly placed penance, but rather letting yourself be submerged in his love, you have a unique place alongside the Suffering Servant. You have the capacity to love him well.

REFLECT

1. Three Suffering Servant Songs are included in the readings for Holy Week (Is 42:1–7; Is 49:1–6; Is 50:4–9). Choose one (or more) and pray with it. Imagine yourself with the Suffering Servant as you pray with the passage.
2. In your prayer, try to think what Jesus must have thought and felt while praying these words himself as a Jewish man and coming to realize that they are about his own Passion ahead.

_____

_____

_____

_____

_____

_____

_____

_____

_____

_____

PRAY

*SUFFERING SERVANT, YOU ENDURED
AGONY TO REDEEM OUR SUFFERING.
SUBMERGE ME IN YOUR LOVE, AND
HELP ME TO EMBRACE WHATEVER
SUFFERING YOU PERMIT ME TO
EXPERIENCE, UNITING IT WITH YOUR
AGONY ON THE CROSS. AMEN.*

HOLY WEEK
HOLY THURSDAY

THE LAST SUPPER IS THE HOUR OF LOVE THAT REACHES TO THE END (AGAPE). LOVE IS THE VERY PROCESS OF PASSING OVER, OF TRANSFORMATION, OF STEPPING OUTSIDE THE LIMITATIONS OF FALLEN HUMANITY—IN WHICH WE ARE ALL SEPARATED FROM ONE ANOTHER AND ULTIMATELY IMPENETRABLE TO ANOTHER— INTO AN INFINITE OTHERNESS.

POPE BENEDICT XVI, *JESUS OF NAZARETH*

THE HOUR OF LOVE

Part of my journey to becoming Catholic included spending lots of time with a very devoted Catholic family. They were intentional about rituals and traditions, one of which included gathering as a family after Holy Thursday Mass to wash one another's feet in memory of what Jesus did for the disciples on Holy Thursday. Every person present washed someone's feet and had their feet washed. The first night I joined them, when it came time for one of my friends to wash my feet, I wept in a way that was foreign to me.

It felt as though I was being transformed in a manner similar to being turned inside out. I felt incredibly vulnerable and humbled; and although it was not a feeling that came naturally to me or felt automatically comfortable, I knew it was good and true. It was true that I needed to receive love, I needed help, I could not make myself clean, I could not heal myself, and I could not become the things I most desired to be all by myself. The changes that needed to happen in me could only be the fruit of agape, the highest form of love: God's own love. This love is only encountered in *other*; it can never be bestowed by oneself, on oneself. What was kicked up in me that evening was the inherent poverty we all have before God, which we can either see as something to resist (Peter exclaims to Jesus in today's gospel, "You shall never wash my feet!" [Jn 13:8]) or as good news (Jesus tells Peter in response that submitting to receiving this gift from Jesus equals inheritance with him). Pope Benedict XVI, in his book *God Is Near Us*, describes Christ's whole life as bending down to wash our feet. I think this includes the sacramental life of the Church, which is in major part born in the upper room we commemorate today.

I have wanted these Thursdays in our Lenten journey to be about practical ways to live Eucharistically. The absolutely most practical things we can do are receive the Body, Blood, Soul, and Divinity of Jesus Christ in the Eucharist and regularly go to Confession. In the sacramental life of the Church, we are turned inside out or right side up. We cannot love like God without the sacraments of the Church. We cannot love to the end without the sacraments of the Church.

REFLECT

1. Pray with the Gospel of John 13:1–15. Imagine yourself there while Jesus is washing the disciples' feet. Perhaps imagine Jesus washing your feet.

2. In your prayer, try to think what Jesus must have thought and felt during this exchange. As his time draws to an end, what is his motivation?

3. Be honest with yourself today about where you are concerning your devotion to the Eucharist and Confession. Beyond Lent, how are you being called to grow in this devotion?

_____

_____

_____

_____

_____

_____

_____

_____

_____

_____

PRAY

*LORD OF ALL, DURING YOUR FINAL
DAYS ON EARTH, YOU TAUGHT US
HOW TO GIVE AND RECEIVE LOVE.
HELP ME RECEIVE THE INHERITANCE
YOU HAVE PROVIDED, AND INCREASE
MY DEVOTION TO THE SACRAMENTS
OF YOUR CHURCH. HAVE YOUR WAY
WITH ME. AMEN.*

HOLY WEEK

GOOD FRIDAY

SINCE THEN WE HAVE A GREAT HIGH PRIEST WHO HAS PASSED THROUGH THE HEAVENS, JESUS, THE SON OF GOD, LET US HOLD FAST OUR CONFESSION. FOR WE HAVE NOT A HIGH PRIEST WHO IS UNABLE TO SYMPATHIZE WITH OUR WEAKNESSES, BUT ONE WHO IN EVERY RESPECT HAS BEEN TEMPTED AS WE ARE, YET WITHOUT SINNING. LET US THEN WITH CONFIDENCE DRAW NEAR TO THE THRONE OF GRACE, THAT WE MAY RECEIVE MERCY AND FIND GRACE TO HELP IN TIME OF NEED.

HEBREWS 4:14–16

IN HIS FLESH

My hope for you this Good Friday is that, when you look at Jesus on the Cross, you will see through the sweat, pain, blood, wounds, and marred face and have it all translate into love.

I've heard it said before that Christ's divinity is hidden on the Cross; I could not disagree more. The image of Christ on the Cross is the supreme divine image that we have. It is only divine power and love that could choose paradoxically to use limitless power and strength to ascend to Jerusalem, and ultimately to death on a cross. Small children are able to grasp this concept of the power of love and virtue revealed in the Cross. I will ask them, "What takes more power, to hit your sibling who is getting on your nerves, or to not?" They shout with rolling eyes, "To *not!*" The divine power of Christ is fully revealed today on the Cross.

What does that mean for us? Once I was praying through the Passion of Christ, and in my prayer, the Blessed Virgin was my companion. As I drew closer to Calvary, in prayer with the scriptures, I became acutely aware of my own brokenness. I experienced for a brief time in prayer deep grief and sadness, and this was ultimately a grace because it made me realize how much I needed Jesus to die for me. All the things that had come to my mind in the prayer, wounds from various points in my life, my patterns of sin, my character defects—I imagined them in my hands and then perceived Mary advising me to nail them to the Cross. Through imaginative prayer, I imagined myself adding these things to the wood of the Cross, and I then perceived a gentle correction from Mary in prayer: "Not *there*; rather, in his flesh." Our sins and brokenness that Jesus bears on the Cross are not borne in the wood, but in his body. It is not the wood that goes into the tomb; it is his body.

I pray today that you can consider on a deep personal level what he has done for you and what he has done for the world.

Today his heart is pierced open, and it will never close again. The all-powerful God, who could have taken any approach to your salvation, chose to save you through death, an open heart, and a throne of mercy inside of it.

REFLECT

1. Pray with the Gospel of John 18:1–19, and continue to follow Jesus closely in your prayer, seeking to love him.
2. What would you like to send into the tomb with Jesus? What are the reasons you need Jesus to die for you?

PRAY

ANIMA CHRISTI

*SOUL OF CHRIST, SANCTIFY ME.
BODY OF CHRIST, SAVE ME. BLOOD
OF CHRIST, EMBOLDEN ME. WATER
FROM THE SIDE OF CHRIST, WASH ME.
PASSION OF CHRIST, STRENGTHEN
ME. O GOOD JESUS, HEAR ME.
WITHIN YOUR WOUNDS HIDE ME.
NEVER PERMIT ME TO BE PARTED
FROM YOU. FROM THE EVIL ENEMY
DEFEND ME. AT THE HOUR OF MY
DEATH CALL ME AND BID ME COME
TO YOU, THAT WITH YOUR SAINTS I
MAY PRAISE YOU FOR AGE UPON AGE.
AMEN.*

HOLY WEEK

HOLY SATURDAY

RISE, LET US LEAVE THIS PLACE.
THE ENEMY LED YOU OUT OF
THE EARTHLY PARADISE. I WILL
NOT RESTORE YOU TO THAT
PARADISE, BUT I WILL ENTHRONE
YOU IN HEAVEN. I FORBADE YOU
THE TREE THAT WAS ONLY A
SYMBOL OF LIFE, BUT SEE I WHO
AM LIFE ITSELF AM NOW ONE
WITH YOU.

**ANCIENT HOMILY FOR HOLY
SATURDAY, CHRIST DEPICTED AS
SPEAKING TO ADAM, FROM THE OFFICE
OF READINGS, LITURGY OF THE HOURS,
NON-BIBLICAL READINGS FOR
LENTEN SEASON**

IN THE HEART OF THE EARTH

On Holy Saturday, the Church teaches that Christ has descended into the earth to bring the fruits of the offering of himself, his espousal to mankind, to those who have died and await him. This means his time in the tomb is good news. What must that mean for the heart of the earth, the heart of the world?

One Good Friday in the novitiate I was listening to a homily given at the Carmelite monastery near our convent by their chaplain. I do not remember what he said, but his words caused a Good Friday image to spring into my mind that has never left. On the surface of Calvary, the sky was dark like night, and rain was falling. The darkness was so thick that the wood of the three crosses appeared black instead of brown. Jesus and the two criminals hung on their crosses, their lives ended. But beneath the surface, below the soil of Calvary, which had been blessed with the blood of Christ, something different was happening. There was a budding springtime from the depths of the earth. Christ's blood seemed to have planted seeds, and even in the destruction of Calvary, the fruits of resurrection were already dawning, like a garden beneath the surface.

John 19:41 reads, "Now in the place where he was crucified there was a garden, and in the garden a new tomb where no one had ever been laid." Today, Jesus is in the depths of the earth, doing something hidden, but that inevitably breaks through the surface, beginning with his Resurrection and being fulfilled in yours. Today, he tends the heart of the earth.

No sacraments are celebrated in the Church during the day on Holy Saturday because for this day it is as if there is no Christ, which would mean no Church, no sacraments. Tabernacles throughout the world will be empty until the evening Vigil Mass, and the Blessed Sacrament has been hidden away in a tabernacle at an altar of repose since Holy Thursday night. There should be no Holy Hours or Adoration; but in the convent, I would notice our elderly Sisters on Holy Saturday quietly slipping into the area of the altar of repose in the convent, to adore Jesus hidden there until we celebrate his Resurrection.

Today, yes, we need to go about as if Jesus is dead; he is, in the flesh. But I invite you to join the Sisters who seek him in the hidden repose, hidden in the depths of the earth, alive and at work, making the heart of the earth fruitful with his loving sacrifice.

REFLECT

1. This Holy Week is about unity with Christ, so for your prayer today, join him in the depths of the earth as he goes first to Adam and Eve. Visit www.vatican.va/spirit/documents/spirit_20010414_omelia-sabato-santo_en.html to read the entire Ancient Homily for Holy Saturday. What might Jesus be thinking and feeling in his descent?
2. Try to spend time outside today. Look for signs of spring. Consider walking barefoot so you can feel the earth beneath you.

PRAY

*ALL-POWERFUL LORD, I AM THE WORK
OF YOUR HANDS, AND YOU HAVE NOT
MADE ME TO BE HELD A PRISONER
IN THE UNDERWORLD. AWAKEN MY
HEART. HELP ME TO RISE WITH YOU
AND GO FORTH, FOR YOU IN ME AND
I IN YOU, TOGETHER, WE ARE ONE
UNDIVIDED PERSON. AMEN.*

HOLY WEEK

EASTER SUNDAY

HOPE DOES NOT DISAPPOINT
US, BECAUSE GOD'S LOVE HAS
BEEN POURED INTO OUR HEARTS
THROUGH THE HOLY SPIRIT WHO
HAS BEEN GIVEN TO US.

ROMANS 5:5

HE IS RISEN INDEED

Thank you for taking this Lenten journey into the wilderness within, then back out, with Jesus on his mission, and to the Cross. It is a tremendous honor that you would give me the trust of walking with you this Lent. On this final day I would like you to complete this journey by praying through the meditation written by St. Ignatius titled "Contemplation to Attain the Love of God" (included in the Reflect section below). It is not as it sounds, as if it is an achievement of God's love, but more accurately is understood as a time of prayer about how you will go forward with God's love as your end and as your purpose. St. Ignatius gives two directives to the people making this prayer before setting them free to pray. One, he notes that love ought to manifest itself in deeds rather than words. And two, he notes that love consists in a sharing of goods; the lover gives and shares with the beloved what he possesses, and vice versa.

At the outset of our journey, you gave Jesus permission to enter your wilderness-like heart to restore order, to rescue you, to tend the garden of your heart, and then to empower you to pour out the fruits of this encounter with him, not only in mission and ministry, but simply in response to his love with your own love back to him. You handed Jesus your heart. You are the beloved, which means he also gave you something of his.

I mentioned as we began that you might be surprised what you would find in your hands come Easter morning. Look down now and see; there you hold Christ's own heart. He is your inheritance (see Psalm 16:6). And "through the Holy Spirit, the love which permeates the Heart of Jesus is poured out in the hearts of men (cf. Romans 5:5), and moves them to adoration of his 'unsearchable riches' (Eph 3:8) and to filial and trusting petition to the Father (cf. Romans 8:15–16) through the Risen One who 'always lives to make intercession for us' (Heb 7:25)" (Letter of

St. John Paul II on the 100th Anniversary of the Consecration of the Human Race to the Divine Heart of Jesus).

You have made this wonderful exchange with Christ; you are in possession of a great treasure. How will you steward the gift of the Resurrection, in deed?

REFLECT

1. Imagine yourself standing before the risen Lord, and allow yourself to call to mind the blessings you have received this Lent and Holy Week.

2. Feel gratitude for all that the Lord has done, and ask God to show you how you are called to, in all things, love and serve the Divine Majesty, who continues to work to make your wilderness within a resurrection garden with God's love enthroned.

_____

_____

_____

_____

_____

_____

_____

_____

_____

PRAY

ADAPTED FROM POPE FRANCIS,
EVANGELII GAUDIUM

*RISEN LORD, FILL ME WITH A NEW
ARDOR BORN OF THE RESURRECTION,
THAT I MAY BRING TO ALL THE
GOSPEL OF LIFE THAT TRIUMPHS
OVER DEATH. GIVE ME A HOLY
COURAGE TO SEEK NEW PATHS SO
THAT THE GIFT OF UNFADING BEAUTY
MAY REACH EVERY HEART. AMEN.*

APPENDIX

IMPLICIT RELIGION
INCOMPLETE SENTENCES
CATHOLIC EDITION, SELF-ADMINISTERED

People have all kinds of feelings, thoughts, desires, attitudes, impulses, and intentions about God, the Blessed Virgin Mary, the Church, and themselves in the spiritual life. Find a quiet place to reflect on these questions, and write your *felt* responses in your own journal. The sentence stems below pull from your emotional experience (which might not seem rational to you). The sentences do *not* seek an intellectually neat, tidy, or "right" catechism answer. This instrument is designed to help you see more clearly what is going on beneath the surface of your religious and spiritual experience and to help you better understand your internal psychological and relational experiences with God, Mary, the Church, and yourself.

1. The closer I feel to Jesus ...

2. God is like my father ...

3. Jesus feels ...

4. My conscience ...

5. My mother and God are similar in ...

6. In my life, God is most focused on ...

7. When I sin, I feel . . .

8. When I receive the Eucharist . . .

9. I am worried that God the Father . . .

10. I misunderstand God when . . .

11. I am angry that God . . .

12. God's warmth and kindness for me . . .

13. When I suffer, God . . .

14. Other Catholics . . .

15. When I am weak, Jesus seems to . . .

16. Jesus wants me to . . .

17. For me, the hardest thing about prayer . . .

18. Jesus likes my . . .

19. I need God to . . .

20. I have trouble understanding why God . . .

21. To me, the Church seems . . .

22. The one way I could change to please God most is . . .

23. In my life, I was closest to God when . . .

24. God's plan for me . . .

25. Souls in hell . . .

26. God the Father allows me . . .

27. I failed God . . .

28. In my life, the Blessed Virgin Mary . . .

29. It is hard for me to believe in God's . . .

30. When I was a young child, God . . .

31. God is most pleased when I . . .

32. At the darkest time of my life, God . . .

33. What needs to change in my relationship with Jesus is . . .

34. In my life, the Holy Spirit . . .

35. When I make mistakes, Jesus . . .

36. I don't understand God's . . .

37. Jesus's love for me . . .

38. My cross is . . .

39. Jesus hates . . .

40. The Church needs . . .

41. I am thankful that God . . .

42. God speaks to me . . .

43. I see Jesus in . . .

44. I wish I never . . .

45. When I pray, I feel . . .

46. Punishment for my sins . . .

47. My relationship with Mary . . .

48. The place I feel closest to God is . . .

49. I yearn for God to . . .

50. Satan tempts me . . .

JUNE JAMESON is an independent artist who creates large oils on canvases for galleries, churches, hospitals, and private collections. Jameson has developed a unique style that blends her strong Catholic faith with her impressionist paintings.

Jameson earned her bachelor of arts degree from the University of Florida. Many of her original paintings are represented by the Sacred Art Gallery in Arizona and several of her images are available to license for liturgical use through the Diocesan Library of Art.

Jameson lives in Ocala, Florida, with her husband and nine children.

Prints of her work, including the images created for *Wilderness Within*, can be found at junejameson.com.

SR. JOSEPHINE GARRETT, CSFN, is a sister of the Holy Family of Nazareth, a licensed counselor, host of the *Hope Stories* podcast, and a Catholic speaker and author.

Garrett earned a bachelor's degree in political philosophy from the University of Dallas. Prior to entering religious life, she worked as vice president in the home loans division of Bank of America. In 2019, she earned a master's degree in clinical mental health counseling from the Chicago School of Professional Psychology and became a nationally certified counselor licensed in Texas.

She worked as a school counselor in Tyler, Texas, and is presently serving as a counselor in private practice. Garrett is a voice for mental health on various platforms such as Formed and Hallow.

She resides in Tyler, Texas.

hopestories.osvpodcasts.com
Instagram: @sr_josephine
Twitter: @sjosephine_CSFN

Let Sr. Josephine Garrett, CSFN Guide You through the 40 Days of Lent with **FREE** *Wilderness Within* Companion Videos and Resources:

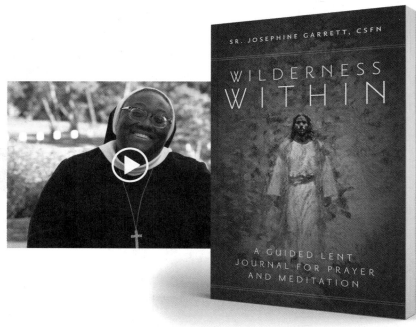

Perfect for individuals, parishes, small groups, and classrooms, these resources include:

- weekly companion videos with Sr. Josephine Garrett, CSFN
- *Wilderness Within Leader's Guide*
- pulpit and bulletin announcements
- downloadable flyers, posters, and digital graphics
- and more!